"Tony Rossell is the Master of Mem
theoretical treatise; it reflects Tony's wo
principles repeatedly to the great benefit of many membership associations. As the
terrain shifts under the feet of non-profit associations, and for-profit corporations
capitalize on the membership model, Tony's expertise on member acquisition and
retention is to be treasured by anybody serious about membership growth."

Ron Mattocks
Chief Operating Officer
Council for Advancement and Support of Education (CASE)

"I have worked with Tony for many years. He has a relentless dedication to the
achievement of an organization's growth goals through his ability to implement
targeted messaging that offers a strong and compelling reason to take action and
his use of data to measure success."

Roger C. Myers, Jr., CPA, MBA
Chief Financial Officer
Certified Financial Planner Board of Standards, Inc.

"If you are in the membership business, do yourself and your organization a favor
by buying and reading this book. Tony Rossell understands the membership
business better than anyone. Save yourself years of trial and error by discovering
what he has learned during a long and successful career in membership marketing.
Tony knows what works today and where the trends are leading us tomorrow."

Frank Kenny
Founder
Chamber Pros Community

"Great associations have great membership programs, period. If I were going to
read only one book on how to develop, nurture, and grow your business,
particularly during these challenging times, it would be this one. Tony has been
the industry expert for the past thirty years, and his knowledge is invaluable."

Chris Strong
Senior Vice President, Conventions and Membership
National Business Aviation Association

"I have had the good fortune to partner with Tony Rossell for the last decade to
double my association's membership, and am always impressed by his ability to
leverage his deep marketing expertise to generate new ideas and strategies to grow
acquisition and retention. You might never be lucky enough to work with Tony, but
if you have the good sense to purchase his book, you will benefit from his lifetime
of experience to gain practical, powerful insights and frameworks that drive
membership growth."

Stephen Fox
Vice President, Membership and Constituent Relations
American Nurses Association

ISBN: 978-1-7362493-0-7
Published by
Marketing General Incorporated
Alexandria, VA
Edited by Kathy Rossell, Bill Schaffner, and Diane Platt
Book design by Nicole Clark and Stella Niblett

Membership Recruitment

How to Grow Recurring
Revenue, Reach New Markets,
and Advance Your Mission

Tony Rossell

DEDICATION

To Kathy, Joseph, Claire, and Ben
and
To my colleagues past and present at Marketing General Incorporated

Soli Deo Gloria

CONTENTS

PART THREE
Sustaining Growth and Resiliency 93

PREFACE

The goal of this book is to answer three critical questions: Why is a growing membership so important? How can a thriving membership program be planned and executed? And, what is required to achieve long-term membership resiliency?

Simply stated, members represent the dynamic force that generates volunteers, customers, attendees, content, and ongoing revenue to enable an association to accomplish its mission. A growing membership is a rising tide that lifts all boats. In the for-profit world, it's recognized that companies decay when they stop growing.

Here is what I have observed from stagnant or declining association membership. A lack of growth results in tighter budgets and limits the development of new initiatives and investment in products and services. At the same time, efficiency decreases as fixed costs are spread over fewer members, often forcing increased prices and higher dues rates. The decline also impacts the members' view of the association. It produces less momentum and excitement. Members may demand lower pricing as they perceive a drop in value or look for alternative providers. For the association staff, as decline sets in, the opportunity for advancement and financial rewards also decreases.

If the impact of the lack of growth is so significant, what is the solution for driving a healthy and robust membership program? While all aspects of the membership relationship—from awareness to engagement to renewal are essential—I will argue in this book that the standalone driver to success is adding more members through an effective membership recruitment program.

How can I make that claim? Isn't it important to engage members or to maintain a high renewal rate? Yes, keeping the members you worked hard to get is necessary, but as we will see from both case studies and research data, growth comes from focused and continuous new member recruitment efforts.

There is an ancient proverb that says, "Without counsel plans fail, but with many advisers, they succeed." So, in addition to sharing my experiences in helping associations grow, I have gathered wisdom from many others. The insights shared here include the best practices learned by my firm in working with hundreds of our clients and partners. I have also used over a decade of feedback that we have received from literally thousands of associations participating in the annual *Membership Marketing Benchmarking Report* survey.

In addition to these sources, I have incorporated the thoughts from both contemporary and past generations of marketing experts. Some of these experts include Sarah Sladek, *The End of Membership as We Know It*; Sheri Jacobs, *The Art of Membership*; and Mark Levin, *Membership Development: 101 Ways to Get and Keep Your Members*. You will find the insights of other contemporary marketers like Robbie Kellman Baxter, Robert Bly, Seth Godin, Philip Kotler, and Simon Sinek reflected in these pages. I have also reached back in time to highlight the wisdom of well-known marketers from the past whose insights are still relevant today, including Bob Stone, Victor Schwab, David Ogilvy, and Claude Hopkins.

Finally, there are a number of ways that you can approach this book. Of course, you are welcome to read it from cover to cover. However, I have purposely presented the content in three sections so that you can focus on specific areas of interest and circle back to others as needed.

The first section makes a case for why membership recruitment is vital to sustain an association and help it to accomplish its mission. The second section gives practical guidance on how a membership recruitment program can be established and optimized to generate more members. This guidance includes defining target markets, delivering value and special offers, making the most of the available marketing channels, creating compelling messaging, and maximizing results through testing. The final section looks at where successful and growing associations should focus their efforts in the future to innovate and continue growth.

The bottom line is that your association can achieve membership growth. Put to use the insights here to help fulfill your organization's mission and impact the people and companies in your marketplace.

ACKNOWLEDGMENTS

Many people over the years have provided guidance, support, and insight to make this book possible. To start, I want to acknowledge the Marketing General Incorporated (MGI) leadership team of Rick Whelan, Raylene Woods, Tom Beauchamp, and Todd Michaels. They have supported and encouraged this effort. Many of the principles in this book were shared with me by the founder of MGI, Scott McBride.

I am also very grateful to Kathy Rossell, who provided ongoing editorial guidance and Diane Platt and Bill Schaffner for proofreading and copyediting. Nicole Clark and Stella Niblett provided the graphic design for the book and Kimberly Humphries oversaw book production. Finally, at the risk of missing some, I want to recognize the colleagues and clients who shared with me their friendship and wisdom. This book includes many of their contributions gained through my interactions from working with them over the years. They include the following, listed in alphabetical order:

Aleda Ahmed, Elisa Joseph Anders, Paula Aviles, Jacklyn Attia, Bill Baldwin, Krista Barnes, Miranda Barrett, Stan Barrett, Jim Brandt, Jack Benson, Rob Bergeron, Betty Berry, Don Blom, Chris Bluhm, Angelyn Boose, Trish Borzon, Kellie Bove, Toni Brearley, Candy Brecht, Bill Brody, Bill Bushaw, Tim Butte, Michael Byrnes, Dawn Caous, Carol Cohen, Jerry Cooper, Mary Beth Cornell, Lorenzo Cowgill, Jana Darling, Jacqueline Davey, Joy Davis, Jim DeGraffenreid, Lisa Diener, Katharine Dixon, Meghan Donohoe, Jim Doyle, Jennifer Durham, Debra Emory, Sally Fackelman, Hisham Fahmy, Joe Fiochetta, Eric Fletty, Scott Fowler, Steve Fox, Linda Gale, Ben Gamse, Barb Gamez, Karen Gebhart, Dori Gedris, Melanie Gibson, Julia Goswick, Alex Graham, Anthony Graziano, Kerri Green, Jeremy Griffin, Susan Griffin, Jason Gudenius, Patrick Haller, Sima Hassassian, Kate Hawley, Conrad Heibel, Ann Henley, Brett Jeffery, Bill Jerome, Un Johnson, Christy Jones, Lori Jordan, Melody Jordan-Carr, Bonnie Kasander, Aimee Kaufman, Matt Kerr, Tom Koerner, Kirby Konz, Addy Kujawa, Vinay Kumar, Kay Lamont, Brian LeHouillier, Catherine Lincoln, Scott MacKenzie, Matthew Mantione,

Simona Marcellus, Walter Marlowe, Ron Mattocks, Harold Mauer, Brian Mazza, Michael McGough, Kelsey McKinney, Greg Melia, Syma Mendelsohn, Mike Meyers, Ron Miletta, Genaro Montanez, Roger Myers, Eric Oyan, Connie Penne, Lina Perez, Frank Peterson, Michelle Peterson, Noah Poissant, Arina Polukhina, Dan Ratner, Neil Reichenberg, Gail Reisman, Marilee Rist, Cynthia Rosso, Becca Rubin, Charles Salvetti, John Sample, Erik Schonher, Scott Seril, Regina Shea, Jacqueline Snyder, Robert Svihla, Christyl Smith, Bob Steventon, Chris Strong, Page Stull, Paula Swann, Joe Syrowik, Dave Taylor, Denise Taylor, Jim Templin, Jim Toner, Rebecca Turner, Jerry Vang, Jeff Ward, Adina Wasserman, Dean West, Charity Westfall, Tom Wilkerson, Meri Beth Wojtaszek, Jacqueline Zeranski

Tony Rossell
January 2021, Alexandria, VA

PART ONE

THE **CHALLENGES** AND **OPPORTUNITIES** OF MEMBERSHIP

CHAPTER ONE

DOES MEMBERSHIP STILL WORK?

Alexis de Tocqueville, a French sociologist, traveled to America in 1831 initially to study the prison system in the United States. However, he was taken by American culture and, upon his return to France, published his classic *Democracy in America in 1835.*[1] One of the enduring observations de Tocqueville made in his writing was the tendency of Americans to band together in various forms of associations. For nearly a thousand years in Europe, membership was common as people came together in craftsman guilds, merchant trade groups, and purpose-driven societies to provide security, to further professional interests, or to advance a cause.

However, in the United States, he found a heightened expression of this association membership tendency. He wrote, "In no country in the world has the principle of association been more successfully used, or more unsparingly applied to a multitude of different objects, than in America. Besides the permanent associations which are established by law under the names of townships, cities, and counties, a vast number of others are formed and maintained by the agency of private individuals." He observed that, "in the United States associations are established to promote public order, commerce, industry, morality, and religion; for there is no end which the human will, seconded by the collective exertions of individuals, despairs of attaining."[2]

For over 150 years in American society, de Tocqueville's observation and indeed the practice of Americans joining together continued to be an accepted cultural norm. However, today, when you look at literature about associations and membership, you can come away with a wholly different

---

[1] Editors, "Alexis de Tocqueville."
[2] Tocqueville and Reeve, *Democracy in America*.

outlook for the future. Many maintain that associations are challenged as never before and call into question the future viability of membership.

The fact that you are reading this book demonstrates that you desire to grow your organization's membership. So, let's first review the concerns some raise about the opportunity to grow. And then explore the case for membership as the driving force to power an association's financial and mission success.

CHALLENGES EMERGING TO MEMBERSHIP

Perhaps the ideas that began to challenge the value and sustainability of membership started first with an article in 1995, and then more fully in 2000, with the publication of *Bowling Alone: The Collapse and Revival of American Community* by Robert D. Putnam, the now-retired professor of Public Policy at Harvard University.

Putnam makes the case that, in earlier days, people bowled in leagues, but no longer, even as the number of people bowling has increased. His example of bowling served as a metaphor for how members of society have increasingly become disconnected from one another and how social structures—whether they be PTA, church, or membership groups like the Elks, Shriners, and Masons—have declined. He notes, for example, that fraternal organizations have witnessed a substantial drop in membership during the 1980s and 1990s. He notes that "after expanding steadily throughout most of this century, many major civic organizations have experienced a sudden, substantial, and nearly simultaneous decline in membership over the last decade or two."[3]

Putnam points to changes ranging from women in the workforce, increased geographic mobility, lower wages, and technology as causing this breakdown in the community. And his theories have become embedded in our cultural view and used as an explanation for declining or stagnant membership.[4]

In truth, associations today do face threats to the membership offerings that they have successfully provided for a hundred years. These obstacles include external threats from changes that are taking place outside of associations' control like web-based information, networking platforms, and the demands of new generations entering the workforce.

Search engines such as Google offer members continuous and immediate access to the information that they seek. Members can network with one another using LinkedIn and other platforms. As one executive

---

[3] "Robert Putnam - Bowling Alone - Journal of Democracy 6:1."
[4] "Putnam, R. D. (1995). Bowling Alone."

from a trade association shared, "Technology makes it easy to get instant answers and educational resources, so we have to evolve and innovate even quicker than before." A *Fast Company* article captured the situation well when talking about how technology is disrupting the association model. "It was once the case that each association owned a small monopoly, providing the single best resource to everyone in their field. No more. With the advent of 24/7 interconnectivity, anyone can set up shop and begin serving your members."[5]

In addition to technology hurdles, associations are faced with understanding and meeting the needs of emerging generations to deliver the value that they are demanding. Sarah Sladek, a writer on the generational impact on associations, captured this challenge well: "Younger people seek and demand a return for membership including tangible member services, high levels of accountability, identifiable career advantages, a sense of professional community, and opportunities to serve within associations."[6] Figuring out how to serve these new generations of potential members has challenged many associations. In a nationwide survey of association executives, one respondent captured the struggle when he shared how inadequate he and his organization felt in how to help "the future workforce and our ability to meet their needs."

Beyond these substantial external challenges, associations also face internal issues to grow their membership. Some associations have accepted the belief that enrollment cannot grow, and rather than risk failure, simply hope to maintain counts or slow the decline in numbers. Others do not invest adequately in marketing because they do not understand the economics of membership. And, some desire to see counts increase, but simply do not have the know-how to move forward with an active membership strategy.

Is there still hope in this day and age to build a
growing membership program? I believe the answer
to that question is a resounding "yes!"

Because of these external threats and internal impediments, some voices say membership no longer works and is "killing associations."[7] Is there still hope in this day and age to build a growing membership program? I believe the answer to that question is a resounding "yes!"

---

[5] Seth Kahan, "6 Key Issues Facing Association Leaders."
[6] Sladek, *End of Membership as We Know It - Building the Fortune-Flipping, Must-Have.*
[7] "Five Reasons Why Membership Is Killing Association Business Models by Jeff De Cagna FRSA FASAE."

MAKING THE CASE FOR MEMBERSHIP GROWTH

There are compelling reasons to believe that a growing membership base can be achieved and that members can be the driving power for association success.

First, and perhaps most important to remember, there remains a deep-seated desire in people to connect around shared interests and values with others, and associations are well-positioned to meet that need. Simon Sinek speaks to this need in his book, *Start with Why: How Great Leaders Inspire Everyone to Take Action.* He says that there is a "very basic human need—the need to belong. Our need to belong is not rational, but it is a constant that exists across all people in all cultures. It is a feeling we get when those around us share our values and beliefs. When we feel like we belong we feel connected and we feel safe. As humans, we crave the feeling and we seek it out."[8]

The truth is not that people no longer want to connect with others, as Putnam maintains, but how they connect has gone through a transformation. For example, while some of the traditional civic organizations are seeing a decline, there is rapid growth for other types of membership organizations ranging from the Humane Society of the United States with 10 million members to AARP with 38 million members. These groups do not base their interaction on face-to-face meetings, but they witnessed extraordinary growth focused around a common cause or value.

Secondly, people's powerful desire to connect with others around value has been ably co-opted by the for-profit world in building customer loyalty through membership programs. Companies are racing to take advantage of and to deploy the membership relationship. In her book, *The Membership Economy*, Robbie Kellman Baxter highlights the potential of the membership model and encourages companies to adopt it: "Membership strengthens loyalty. Membership strengthens participation. Membership strengthens referrals. And organizations that think about membership tend to focus more on providing long-term value, which ultimately leads to better customer lifetime value. Any CEO who is not thinking about membership is missing a huge opportunity to point his or her organization toward long-term sustainable profitability."[9]

The *Harvard Business Review* (HBR) concurs with this strategy. It reports that the continuity or subscription approach is now becoming a more regular practice even in the retail industry because it meets two essential customer needs—convenience and simplifying the many choices that a customer has walking into a store. HBR says that retailers who

---

[8] Sinek, *Start with Why.*
[9] Baxter, *The Membership Economy.*

establish a membership program "forge deeper relationships with customers, gain access to valuable consumer demographic data, tap a recurring revenue stream, and meet growing consumer demand for both convenience and curation."[10] These same membership approaches that are being recommended and effectively working in the for-profit world are the strategies that, unfortunately, some are questioning for associations today.

One does not need to look far for examples of membership models deployed with outstanding success. The list of the for-profit world adopting and growing with the membership model is extensive, with some of the most notable being among familiar household names:

- Amazon Prime has reached 101 million members.[11]
- Netflix now has 139 million members worldwide. [12]
- Costco continues to see steady membership growth with over 94 million members.[13]

Harley Davidson has established the Harley Owners Group (HOG). HOG offers a tiered membership structure with options for full membership, associate membership, and life membership. Benefits include a magazine, newsletter, meetings, and membership discounts. Full membership costs $45 a year, and individuals can even sign up for an annual automatic credit card renewal.[14] All this should sound very familiar to a traditional professional association. Impressively, HOG membership has achieved about one million members and expanded worldwide. Members can select from 680 chapters in the U.S. and over 700 chapters in nearly 100 countries around the world.[15]

Membership can also successfully reach out to and interest younger generations. Nintendo has proven this. Nintendo Switch Online membership offers its young fans an automatically renewing individual membership for $12.99 per year and a family membership for $34.99. The latest reports say that Nintendo has reached 9.8 million members.[16]

Your membership may not achieve the counts that these consumer-based companies reach. But their success demonstrates that people, just like your potential members, will commit to joining your organization when it offers value, community, and resources. As one author put it, "Memberships seem to be everywhere. It's easy to see why. They drive 'forever transactions,' those incredibly valuable customer relationships in

---

[10] Randall, Lewis, and Davis, "How Subscriptions Are Creating Winners and Losers in Retail."
[11] "Amazon Prime Has 100 Million U.S. Members."
[12] "Netflix Grows Subscriber Base to 139 Million Worldwide."
[13] "Costco Membership Worldwide 2018."
[14] "H.O.G. Member Benefits | Harley-Davidson USA."
[15] Galvin, "Harley Owners Group 30th Anniversary Celebration."
[16] "Memberships | Nintendo Switch Online | Nintendo."

which people sign up once but pay again and again, often without considering alternatives."[17]

Thirdly, beyond the for-profit world, and in contradiction to those prophesying the end of associations, data shows that membership remains a very useful and powerful relationship-builder. The association membership model continues to thrive. As Mark Twain famously said on learning of the publication of his obituary, "the report of my death is greatly exaggerated."

The most compelling evidence of the strength of association membership comes from data provided directly from professional and trade association executives.

Over the past decade, survey results show that nearly
half of professional and trade associations reported that
their membership had increased from the previous year.
On the other hand, on average, only 25 percent of associations
said that their membership counts had declined.

The *Membership Marketing Benchmarking Report* has presented survey results gathered each year from nearly 1,000 associations to capture the status of their membership and what practices are working in their marketing efforts. The data shows a remarkable track record demonstrating the vibrancy and continued strength of the association membership model. Over the past decade, survey results show that nearly half of professional and trade associations reported that their membership had increased from the previous year. On the other hand, on average, only 25 percent of associations said that their membership counts had declined.

One exception to this pattern of growth was the fallout from the Great Recession in 2009. However, even during this time of economic dislocation, benchmarking showed that over a third of professional and trade associations still reported that their membership increased. And 42 percent said that they improved their new member input. Additionally, the results from the research in the time shortly after the Great Recession highlighted that membership counts made a remarkable recovery. Following the economic downturn, the proportion of associations reporting increased membership rose rapidly to 50 percent and higher in the subsequent years. Each of the four years after the Great Recession also produced some of the most outstanding new member recruitment results. Just three years after the low point, an all-time high of 63 percent of

---

[17] Baxter, *The Forever Transaction*.

associations said that their new member acquisition had increased year over year.

MEMBERSHIP CHANGE IN PAST YEARS (TREND)

	Increased	Decreased	Remained the same	Not sure
2020	42%	27%	30%	2%
2019	45%	26%	28%	1%
2018	48%	25%	26%	2%
2017	46%	25%	28%	1%
2016	49%	22%	27%	1%
2015	46%	24%	28%	2%
2014	53%	27%	16%	4%
2013	52%	31%	16%	1%
2012	52%	29%	16%	3%
2011	49%	34%	16%	2%
2010	36%	48%	14%	3%
2009	45%	35%	16%	5%

For those associations concerned with the cost of growing membership, there is a foundational economic argument for why to support and fund a growth effort based on the concept of lifetime member value. Membership is a continuity product. Year after year, members pay dues to renew. Some will remain a member for only one year, but the vast majority will continue their membership for multiple years. This ongoing revenue stream can be calculated by multiplying the dues amount by the typical tenure of a member.

An Example of Calculating Lifetime Value:

LIFETIME VALUE

defines the economic value produced by a typical member.

ANNUAL AVERAGE DUES REVENUE PER MEMBER

ANNUAL AVERAGE NON-DUES REVENUE PER MEMBER

AVERAGE TENURE

Using reported average data from the *Membership Marketing Benchmarking Report*, typical lifetime value can be calculated.

In the report, the average individual membership association received $175 in annual dues revenue from a member. The mean renewal rate for a member came to 80 percent. This renewal rate translates to an average tenure or length of membership of five years. Based on these numbers, the revenue stream or lifetime dues value of a member is a substantial sum of $875 ($175 x 5). Members for most associations also represent the most profitable customers. If we assume an average of $50 a year of non-dues purchases for conference attendance, professional development registrations, or publication purchases, then the lifetime value of a member in this example jumps to $1,125.

When an association calculates the lifetime value of a member, then many of the financial concerns with prioritizing and budgeting to acquire and keep members is seen in a new context. Building membership is an investment that produces revenue from dues and purchases for years to come.

Finally, beyond the economic considerations, probably the most significant argument for a vibrant and growing membership is that membership helps an association accomplish its mission. For virtually every association, both individual members and member companies supply the volunteer leadership, the conference speakers, the content producers, the standards writers, and the voice behind issue advocacy. In short, members create the value provided by the association to move the mission forward.

As you will see, there are great opportunities today to build a strong association member base. In sum, membership continues to work and makes sense to support and fund because:

- People continue to be motivated to connect around shared interests and values
- Membership programs have a track record of success with both the for-profit world and non-profit world
- Membership supports the long-term financial health and mission of an association.

In light of the vital role of membership to associations, the goal of this book is to serve as a guide to help address the structural and knowledge issues holding back membership growth. Each chapter shares step-by-step strategies and tactics to build a successful membership program. There are many examples in this book of associations that have effectively grown membership and thrived, but as a starting point, let's look at just one association—the Society for Human Resource Management (SHRM).

CHAPTER TWO

THE BUILDING BLOCKS
OF MEMBERSHIP

In 1990, the Society for Human Resource Management (SHRM) claimed 45,000 HR executives as members. The association's membership had been stable for years and additional revenue came from regular dues increases. At that time, Mike Losey, SPHR, CAE, was selected as the new president and CEO. He decided that budget increases would no longer be supported through dues increases but rather through membership growth.

An aggressive membership recruitment program was put in place with an agency partner. SHRM maintained an industry-standard renewal rate but drove growth by increasing new member input each year. By 1998, during its 50th Anniversary celebration, SHRM announced a milestone of more than 90,000 members worldwide[18]. By 2015, despite changes in technology, HR regulations, and two recessions, SHRM continued membership growth and was ranked the twelfth largest association in the United States with 275,000 human resource and business executive members, bringing in $114.56 million in revenue.[19] By 2019, SHRM membership stood at over 300,000, with 575 chapters in the United States and across 165 countries. Overall, SHRM achieved an average annual membership growth rate of 22 percent since 1990.

What were the ingredients of SHRM's outstanding growth record? At a fundamental level, SHRM simply delivered incredible value to a specific market. SHRM offers the traditional member benefits of a magazine, newsletters, and a portfolio of topic-targeted conferences. However, beyond these, perhaps the most valuable benefit to members is the "Ask an HR Advisor" service where members can call, chat, or email a human resources expert to get answers to their questions and problems.

---

[18] "World's Largest HR Association Reaches Quarter Million Members."
[19] "Society for Human Resource Management."

Statistically, the members who take advantage of this exclusive service are much more likely to remain long-term members of the association.

On top of providing outstanding value to members, SHRM has, for years, run a best practices membership marketing program. From recruitment to engagement to renewal, SHRM tests, tracks, analyzes, and adapts its marketing efforts. Membership recruitment has been a particularly significant driver of success. To maintain growth, SHRM adds nearly 60,000 new members a year using a broad range of marketing channels, including direct mail, email, digital ads, and telemarketing. SHRM has even built market awareness with television ads.

Can this level of growth take place for other associations? The answer is yes. Proportionately, there are associations experiencing membership growth rates at an even faster pace than SHRM, and any association can apply the strategies that drive this growth.[20]

The ingredients that produce this dynamic level of growth for associations are: (1) providing value to members, and (2) communicating that value through each of the stages of the membership relationship. Let's look at each of these ingredients to growth.

START BY PROVIDING OUTSTANDING VALUE

No organization's membership program will succeed without delivering real value to members. Value drives why members stay with an organization, and lack of value is the top reason why they leave. In the *Membership Marketing Benchmarking Report*, association executives also shared how compelling they believed their value proposition was to members. Not surprisingly, associations reporting increases in their membership numbers were significantly more likely to say that they offered members a compelling value proposition.

As one survey respondent commented: "Value, value, value!! If you have it, people will want it. Value has to be real and tangible in a way that people can't compete without it. Slick marketing campaigns and playing with the membership model will never work for associations with little value."

Whether consciously or unconsciously, a member has a simple equation in mind when determining if an association offers the value that he or she desires:

---

[20] In the 12th annual edition of the *Membership Marketing Benchmarking Report*, nearly half of the associations said that their membership had increased over the past five years. Of those associations, 43 percent noted that their membership had increased from 11 percent to 50 percent. And a total of 12 percent saw increases in membership counts of over 50 percent during the previous five-year period.

"What will I get from membership" – (minus) "How much money and time will membership cost" = The Membership Value.[21]

In the landmark ASAE publication *The Decision to Join,* current members, lapsed members, and "never members" from 18 associations were surveyed to help identify the value they were seeking from their membership. When asked about the membership benefits that were or would be the most important in their decision process, the clear winners were:

- Gaining access to the most critical up-to-date information available in the field
- Finding professional development and educational program offerings
- Obtaining opportunities to network with other professionals in their field [22]

More recent research confirms these findings with the exception that for trade associations, advocacy also rates very high as a membership value.

The good news is that most associations are delivering significant value to their members, as evidenced by their renewal rates. Each year, the vast majority of association members are willing to pay their dues in exchange for the value that they are receiving. Association marketing, however, is strengthened by accurately defining the value provided and effectively promoting it. If there is a lack of clarity of what prospective and current members are seeking from an association, research is the appropriate tool to uncover the needs and wants of members. The two important research questions to help understand the value members are seeking and finding with their membership are:

- How important is a given product or service to the member?
- How well does the organization deliver these benefits?

With a better understanding of benefits, products can be evaluated and tailored to meet the needs of members. The services that research shows are most valuable and well-delivered deserve the additional investment of time and resources. They are the core of an association's value proposition. Benefits that are important to members, but are not well delivered, for any number of reasons, require investment to improve them. And benefits that are lower rated can be set aside or eliminated.

---

[21] Jacobs, *Membership Essentials.*

[22] Dalton et al., *The Decision to Join*.

COMMUNICATE MEMBERSHIP VALUE
THROUGH THE MEMBERSHIP LIFECYCLE

In addition to providing tangible value, the second ingredient for membership success is establishing an effective marketing system to communicate value at each stage of the membership relationship.

In the 1989 film, *Field of Dreams*, Ray Kinsella, an Iowa corn farmer, hears a voice telling him: "If you build it, they will come." He interprets this as an instruction to build a baseball diamond on his farm. Once he completes the diamond, baseball players from the past emerge from the cornfields to play ball, and the movie ends with a line of cars filled with fans heading to the field to watch them. The prediction of the voice was fulfilled.

However, while the philosophy of "if you build it, they will come" may be compelling in the movies, it does not work for membership recruitment. Marketers assign products into two basic categories: "pull" and "push" products. A pull product is something in high demand like the hot Christmas toy or the latest tech gadget for which customers line up at the store when it is released. Similarly, coffee drinkers do not need the prodding of an advertisement to remind them to get their morning brew. They seek it out.

Membership, in contrast, is a push product. It is sold, not sought. It is unlikely that any association has a line of prospects or members waiting for them at the office door each morning to join or renew. The failure of associations to recognize this dynamic is why some value-rich associations are member-poor. For membership success, a systematic relationship marketing structure needs to be in place to achieve membership growth. Creating exceptional value without a plan to get the word out is like cooking a wonderful meal for a dinner party but forgetting to invite guests to come over and enjoy it.

For membership success, a systematic relationship marketing structure needs to be in place to achieve membership growth.

A time-tested relationship marketing system for associations is a framework called the membership lifecycle. The membership lifecycle segments the membership experience into five consecutive stages that help an association to diagnose what areas of the membership relationship need attention and to speak to prospects and members based on where they are in the relationship.

Each of the stages is important and needs a high level of competency to maintain and grow an association's membership. However, when looking to build a membership base, as highlighted by SHRM's example, one phase of the lifecycle stands out as the primary driver of success—membership recruitment.

Before focusing on this crucial element, however, let's briefly walk through the stages of awareness, recruitment, engagement, renewal, and reinstatement that make up the membership lifecycle.

Awareness – When Prospects First Discover You

The first step in the membership lifecycle is establishing awareness. No individual or company joins a membership organization unless they know that it exists and provides value that will help them meet a need in their interests, career, or industry.

Consumer brands like Coca-Cola, Kleenex, or Hershey's Kisses define awareness as gaining share of mind so the consumer will recall their product when making a purchasing decision. However, since associations are not reaching out to a broad consumer market but are instead concentrating on a very targeted market of individuals and companies, they have a different awareness goal. Their goal is mutual awareness.

Mutual awareness occurs when an association has established both share of mind and share of database. In other words, an association wants potential members to know who they are, and at the same time, they want to have contact information to reach out to prospects directly.

Building awareness can come from a variety of sources. Many associations report that their top source for awareness is through word of mouth of their members. With the multiplication of information and networking choices, prospective members often turn to colleagues, friends, and faculty for guidance on where to find the solutions that they need. As Philip Kotler maintains in his book, *Marketing 4.0*, "today's customers have become highly dependent on the opinions of others. In many cases, others' words have even outweighed both personal preferences and marketing communications."[23]

Awareness options, more directly controlled by associations, are content marketing and social media. Using these channels, an association can offer a free whitepaper or newsletter, or attendance at a webinar or meeting. As a potential member clicks on a post or ad and accepts one of these content offers, they opt-in and give permission to receive continuing communications from an association. The association is trading content for contact information.

---

[23] Kotler, Kartajaya, and Setiawan, *Marketing 4.0*.

When both the share of mind and share of the database are in place, an association has established mutual awareness so that two-way communication can begin to build toward an ongoing relationship.

Recruitment – When Prospects Choose to Join You

For all associations, there is a constant need for new members. Even for groups that are value-laden and have a high level of member commitment, a portion of an association's membership will leave each year because of retirement, mergers and acquisitions, and companies deciding that they will no longer pay membership dues. You need to replace these members.

Yet, just replacing the members who leave will not result in growth. Growth is driven by adding substantially more members than an association loses each year.

Therefore, associations that want to see an increase in membership counts need to put in place a proactive recruitment plan to acquire new members. A successful recruitment program must address five strategic issues:

1. Understanding who is the target market that the association wants to reach.
2. Determining what membership package to present to potential members and what special offers will encourage a prospect to respond to a promotion.
3. Defining how to reach prospective members through the many marketing channels available, ranging from direct mail to digital advertising.
4. Creating messages on why a member should join an association.
5. Developing where a membership marketing program should go in the future through testing, tracking, and analysis.

Because of the importance of these membership recruitment strategies, each will be explored in-depth in part two of this book.

Engagement – When Members Feel They Belong with You

Something that surprises many association executives is that once a member joins, he or she immediately becomes the most likely member not to renew. Almost all associations report that first-year members have the lowest renewal rates. However, any member who is not using the benefits provided by the association is also at risk for not continuing their membership.

So, the goal of the engagement phase of the lifecycle for new members and those not taking advantage of the value provided by the association is to generate interaction and motivate involvement. Any type of interactive engagement, whether it is a purchase, a visit to the website, a completed survey, or even a phone call by the member to the organization, correlates positively with the ultimate renewal of a member.

A brand-new member is effectively sampling an association's membership, so the need for getting interaction and usage of the association's benefits is particularly vital. That is why engagement starts with new member onboarding that includes a step-by-step guide to orient a new member on how to take advantage of the benefits that they have just signed up to receive. Onboarding plans often include emailed and mailed welcome kits that provide a user manual to members, membership cards and certificates, and an invitation to a new member webinar. Trade associations are also more likely to use volunteer or staff welcome calls to introduce members to the association.

Engaging members does not end with the onboarding process. Just like any friendship, building a relationship requires ongoing communication. Members need continual reminders on what the association includes in their membership and how to use the services to keep them engaged. How critical are these reminders? Association benchmarking data highlights the fact that 73 percent of associations who have seen an increase in renewal rates over the past year have an active program to increase engagement.[24]

It is also essential to understand that how members engage with an association is evolving. Traditionally, membership engagement relied on the three-legged stool of volunteerism, insurance that required continued membership, and attendance at local or regional events. The latest survey data shows that how members engage has gone through a transition.

The research highlights that volunteerism and purchasing association-sponsored insurance are now some of the least engaging platforms. Similarly, the traditional volunteer-run monthly dinner meeting is no longer the primary way participation takes place. Instead, mobile app usage, participation in public and private social networks, attendance at webinars, and visits to the members-only sections of association websites are among the fastest-growing ways that members interact.[25]

---

[24] Rossell, Wasserman, and Kerr, "The Membership Marketing Benchmarking Report."
[25] Rossell, Wasserman, and Kerr.

CHANGES IN MEMBER PARTICIPATION

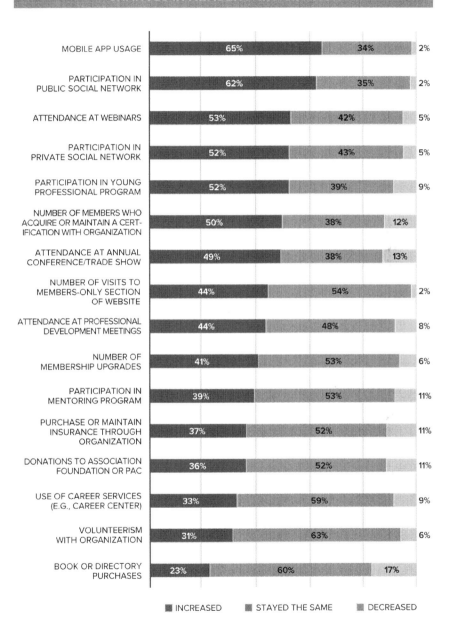

	INCREASED	STAYED THE SAME	DECREASED
MOBILE APP USAGE	65%	34%	2%
PARTICIPATION IN PUBLIC SOCIAL NETWORK	62%	35%	2%
ATTENDANCE AT WEBINARS	53%	42%	5%
PARTICIPATION IN PRIVATE SOCIAL NETWORK	52%	43%	5%
PARTICIPATION IN YOUNG PROFESSIONAL PROGRAM	52%	39%	9%
NUMBER OF MEMBERS WHO ACQUIRE OR MAINTAIN A CERTIFICATION WITH ORGANIZATION	50%	38%	12%
ATTENDANCE AT ANNUAL CONFERENCE/TRADE SHOW	49%	38%	13%
NUMBER OF VISITS TO MEMBERS-ONLY SECTION OF WEBSITE	44%	54%	2%
ATTENDANCE AT PROFESSIONAL DEVELOPMENT MEETINGS	44%	48%	8%
NUMBER OF MEMBERSHIP UPGRADES	41%	53%	6%
PARTICIPATION IN MENTORING PROGRAM	39%	53%	11%
PURCHASE OR MAINTAIN INSURANCE THROUGH ORGANIZATION	37%	52%	11%
DONATIONS TO ASSOCIATION FOUNDATION OR PAC	36%	52%	11%
USE OF CAREER SERVICES (E.G., CAREER CENTER)	33%	59%	9%
VOLUNTEERISM WITH ORGANIZATION	31%	63%	6%
BOOK OR DIRECTORY PURCHASES	23%	60%	17%

Renewal – When Current Members Decide Whether to Keep You

Whenever an election season starts, a flood of mailings, phone calls, online ads, and emails will begin encouraging voters to support this candidate or that candidate. Politicians know that just sending one letter or making one phone call is not a strategy that will maximize voter turnout and get them elected. So, they are very aggressive (most say too aggressive) in turning out the vote for themselves.

In the same way, the renewal portion of the membership lifecycle is about keeping the growth already earned by an association through their awareness, recruitment, and engagement efforts and getting the member to "vote" to continue with the association. That is why there is a practical application for associations to adapt the political campaign mindset. The minimalist three-part renewal series that organizations have deployed for years is no longer enough to maximize retention rates. Instead, associations are using multi-channel, high-frequency approaches to reach members with direct mail, email, telephone calls, online ads, and, even in some cases, texting to be sure that the renewal message gets through.

These multiple contacts can help address one of the top reasons reported for non-renewal—the member simply forgot. As one membership director shared, "We heard from many lapsed members that they simply didn't know it was time to renew." Add to that the inertia that everyone experiences from time to time, and it is apparent that we need to provide additional pushes to gain renewals.

RENEWAL RATE

measures the number of members kept over a given period of time (Usually a fiscal or calendar year).

TOTAL NUMBER OF CURRENT MEMBERS   NEW MEMBERS IN THE PAST 12 MONTHS   TOTAL NUMBER OF MEMBERS IN THE PREVIOUS YEAR

Reinstatement – When Former Members Agree to Return to You

In life, there will always be bumps in the road with any relationship. It is no different in the membership relationship. However, it almost always makes more sense to try and restore an existing connection than to start a new one. The reinstatement portion of the lifecycle (also known as a membership winback) is where lapsed member recovery takes place.

There are several excellent reasons why associations should focus their attention on trying to reinstate former members. First, former members are aware of the association's benefits. There is not a need to educate them from scratch. Secondly, former members' previous behavior identifies them as individuals who, at one point in time, had an interest in and need for what the association has to offer. Finally, for recently lapsed members, the association has the contact information and an established business relationship allowing it to reach out through a variety of channels, including email, phone, and direct mail.

What's more, many associations find that former members are often up to five times more likely to respond to a membership offer than those who have never been members. The for-profit marketplace has found this same high level of responsiveness. In the article "Winning Back Lost Customers" published in the *Harvard Business Review*, data was gathered from winback efforts for telecom customers. The analysis showed that firms are better off shifting more time and money to getting former customers to come back than relying solely on new customer recruitment efforts.[26]

One additional advantage of implementing a reinstatement program is that it is a quality control check on an association's renewal program. Ironically, the good news is that if former members do not come back, it means that the association's renewal efforts are airtight and working effectively. However, most associations find that they get a strong response from their reinstatement efforts. This level of response indicates that renewal efforts are not as effective as they could be and need some attention.

NEXT STEPS

Safely driving a car requires keeping an eye on the dashboard to make sure you have enough fuel, looking at the rearview and side mirrors to see what is coming up from behind, and checking signs and GPS for

---

[26] "Winning Back Lost Customers."

directions. However, to safely reach the destination, the most serious job is keeping one's eyes focused on the road ahead.

The same is true for a membership program. For a growing membership, an organization needs some essential ingredients, including providing outstanding products and services that fuel membership value, making sure members are engaged, and tracking the direction of renewals to maintain a hard-earned membership base. Nevertheless, focusing on the road ahead to find and recruit new members is the most powerful lever for growing membership.

Compared to any other single marketing initiative, a thriving recruitment effort will enable an association to increase its revenue, expand its market reach, and advance its mission. Let's next look at why recruitment is so critical.

CHAPTER THREE

THE POWER OF
MEMBERSHIP RECRUITMENT

In their book, *The One Thing: The Surprising Simple Truth Behind Extraordinary Results*, Gary Keller and Jay Papasan make the case that by trying to do everything well, we do nothing great. Instead, they say, narrowing one's focus on the one high leverage opportunity results in outstanding success.

To demonstrate the point, the authors highlighted a paper published in the *American Journal of Physics* on domino falls and the cascading effect of knocking over one domino in a line of dominos. The *Journal* reported on the experiment of how domino falls amplify in power. "A single domino is capable of bringing down another domino that is actually 50 percent larger."[27] The power of the falling dominos grows in a geometric progression, so ultimately a single domino knocked over can topple a substantial structure.

RESEARCH HIGHLIGHTS THE IMPACT
OF MEMBERSHIP RECRUITMENT

As described in the previous chapter, there are many ingredients to establishing a robust membership program; however, "the one thing" that most supports membership growth is adding new members to the top of the membership funnel.

---

[27] Keller and Papasan, *The One Thing.*

It's said that "a rising tide raises all boats," and new
members for an association represent that rising tide.

For many, this emphasis on recruitment may sound heretical. Isn't it a marketing dogma that it is more expensive to acquire a new member than to renew an existing one? At one level, this is true. Gaining new members is more challenging and costly than keeping an existing one. But years of survey data and some relatively simple calculations make the case that you cannot renew your membership into growth. It's said that "a rising tide raises all boats," and new members for an association represent that rising tide.

The data from survey results in the *Membership Marketing Benchmarking Report* strongly support the positive impact of membership recruitment. As noted earlier, over the past decade, nearly half of associations reported membership counts increased at twice the rate of those that had a decline in their membership. Remarkably, one statistic that has remained constant over the past decade is the reported level of membership renewals. Individual membership associations' average renewal rates have not varied by more than a point or two from 80 percent. Substantially improving the renewal rate for a competently managed retention program has not been something that associations have achieved.

If membership counts are increasing and the growth has not been the result of improved renewal performance, what has been the driver of this growth? The answer is new member acquisition. Going back over the past ten years, nearly half of the associations have reported that their new member acquisition has increased.[28] As this increased number of new members has flowed in, simultaneously, total counts have gone up.

As further evidence of the effect of recruitment on total membership counts, survey results show associations with an increase in new members acquired are significantly more likely also to show an increase in total membership counts over the last five-year period. And associations that reported declines in new member acquisition saw a drop in their full membership.[29] In short, associations are not renewing but, instead, recruiting themselves into growth.

---

[28] The latest benchmarking research continues this decade-long trend of stable renewal rates and growth driven by new member acquisition. Average renewal rates remain static at 82 percent while 45 percent of associations report seeing an increase in new member acquisition. Overall, 42 percent of associations say that total membership increased for the year.

[29] Rossell, Wasserman, and Kerr, "The Membership Marketing Benchmarking Report."

CALCULATING THE IMPACT OF
MEMBERSHIP RECRUITMENT

There is a calculation to demonstrate the impact membership recruitment has on overall membership counts. The method is called a Steady State Analysis. The concept of a steady state calculation can be illustrated with a person's weight gain or loss. When the calories consumed by a person remains stable, and the calories burned through activity and exercise are constant, a person's weight will ultimately arrive at an equilibrium or steady state. It will no longer increase or decrease unless there is a change in diet or exercise.

The same is true with an association's membership counts. If the new member input and the number of members lapsing remain constant, an association's membership will reach equilibrium where the number of new members matches the number of members lost. The organization will hit a steady state. This calculation works no matter where the starting point is of an organization's total membership. It is solely driven by how many members leave and how many are added.

How to Calculate Steady State

STEADY STATE ANALYSIS

defines the equilibrium of total membership at which point members gained will offset members lost.

ANNUAL NEW   LAPSE
MEMBER INPUT   RATE

To calculate the steady state of an organization's membership requires two numbers: the current annual new member input and the organization's lapse rate (non-renewal rate) shown as a decimal. Divide the new member input by the lapse rate and the result shows the future membership outcome if the status quo is maintained.

The formula is Annual New Member Input / Reciprocal of Renewal Rate (or Lapse Rate) Shown as a Decimal = Total Membership Steady State.

For example, with an annual input of 1,000 New Members and a .25 Lapse Rate, the steady state of membership will be 4,000.

This steady state calculation works no matter where the starting point is of an organization's total membership. It is driven by how many members leave and how many are added.

The steady state calculation models the long-term impact of an association's changes in membership recruitment and retention rate. Here are three sample scenarios showing the outcome in total members with higher renewal rates and fewer new members and lower renewal rates and increased new members.

- In the first scenario, an association maintains an 85 percent renewal rate and has a new member input of 500 per year. This steady state calculation results in an outcome of 3,333 total members.
- In the second scenario, an association maintains an 82 percent renewal rate and has a new member input of 1,000 per year. This steady state calculation results in an outcome of 5,555 total members.
- In the third scenario, an association maintains an 80 percent renewal rate and has a new member input of 2,000 per year. This steady state calculation results in an outcome of 10,000 total members.

These scenarios help to demonstrate the challenge of membership growth solely through increasing retention rates compared to the potential through increasing new member input. In the last calculation, even factoring in a possible diminished renewal rate, increasing the new member input resulted in a substantially higher total membership outcome. A steady state calculation makes it clear that an increase in membership recruitment can drive overall membership growth.

The natural follow-up questions from the steady state analysis then become whether this increase in recruitment can be achieved and, if so, how to accomplish it. What follows is an example of how one association has demonstrated that substantial increases in membership recruitment drive total membership growth.

HOW INCREASING MEMBERSHIP
RECRUITMENT CHANGED ONE ASSOCIATION

The American Nurses Association (ANA) is the premier professional association representing the interests of the nation's registered nurses through joint membership with affiliated state nurses' associations. In just over five years, ANA has grown membership by 61 percent, with annual growth rates ranging from 6 percent to 9 percent.[30]

However, for years, a growing membership was not the norm for ANA. In fact, by 2011, ANA membership had declined from well over 100,000

---

[30] "Member Acquisition."

members to 90,000 members due to the disaffiliation of five of ANA's state associations and inconsistent membership marketing efforts.

ANA leadership realized that significant changes were needed to reverse the membership decline and stop the hemorrhaging. The board, executive director, and membership vice president set a goal for ANA to become a high-growth membership organization. The two decisions to accomplish this change were to focus on improving the membership value proposition and allocating significant budget dollars for an ongoing membership recruitment effort.

Additionally, the membership team at ANA committed to function as a "learning organization" to identify innovations in membership marketing, aggressively test them, measure and analyze the results, and then deploy them in the recruitment efforts. To help accomplish these goals, ANA decided to partner with a direct response agency to add to their capabilities and expertise.

To improve the value proposition and bring better alignment between the price and membership benefits, ANA launched a program with their state nurses' associations to offer a reduced-price standard membership category for new members. At the same time, existing members received additional benefits through a new category called Premier membership. Through these multi-level membership categories, ANA was able to present an economical membership option to potential new members without sacrificing revenue growth from the loyal current membership base.

Concurrently with enhancing membership value, ANA launched a membership recruitment program built around market testing and analysis. ANA's testing efforts included:

- Tests of creative to determine what messages, copy, and graphics are most effective;
- Audience tests to find the best market segments and prospect lists;
- Special offer tests to identify the incentives that encourage a prospect to join; and
- Marketing channel tests to properly allocate budgets for direct mail, email, online advertising, and telemarketing.

The outcome of the testing resulted in an integrated channel, multi-touch recruitment program. The annual marketing efforts featured six recruitment campaigns each year. These campaigns include direct mail to former members and contacts in the ANA database, along with rented third-party lists and multiple emails. Results showed that when email efforts were sent simultaneously with direct mail, both channels saw improvement.

Additionally, ANA ran paid digital advertising continually throughout the year. The most effective ads drove prospects directly to the ANA join page and annually have produced up to 5,000 new paid members. The digital program has advertised on Google, LinkedIn, and Facebook.

Digital ads on Facebook were particularly effective for ANA to recruit new members.[31] The online techniques included using Facebook custom audience ads that showed ads to an uploaded list of prospects who were also receiving direct mail and email membership offers. ANA also found success with Facebook lookalike ads that display invitations to candidates who look like current ANA members. Retargeting ads to prospects that visited the ANA website but had not made the decision to join produced outstanding results.

Another major step to enhance marketing effectiveness was to build a prospect database and score potential members on their likelihood to join based on their previous behavior, original source, and demographics. Those individuals with a high score received the full complement of marketing efforts. However, for those individuals who were much less likely to join, they only received lower-cost marketing efforts like an email or digital ad.

To continue to accelerate growth, ANA also launched a successful early career membership campaign to reach younger nurses. Like many other associations, ANA tends to have members in their 40's and 50's. ANA used content marketing to build an early career prospect list by offering a "new to the profession" welcome kit. Early career members also received a substantial discount on dues, a private online community, and had access to a mentor program.[32]

Through this strategy of focusing on value and then funding and executing a sophisticated recruitment program, ANA overcame its steep membership decline and established a sustainable program resulting in an increase in membership from 90,000 to more than 150,000.[33]

Because ANA had already established such a powerful membership marketing infrastructure when the COVID-19 pandemic hit along with the subsequent recession, the association was able to adapt the tools that it had created to meet the critical needs of members and the nursing community. For example, ANA developed a free COVID-19 webinar series and made it available at no charge to both members and nonmembers. They promoted the webinar series via email and paid digital advertising and drew over 190,000 registrations. By meeting the needs of nurses during this time, ANA also experienced a dramatic rise in new members.

[31] "Member Acquisition."
[32] "Is Career Stage the Key to Member Acquisition?"
[33] Carol Cohen and Elisa Joseph, "Membership CPR: From Flagging to Thriving in Just 5 Years."

Membership grew by 12 percent in April and May of 2020, with over 23,000 new joins.[34] This increase represented the highest new member recruitment levels in the history of the organization.

How can your organization develop a program to drive membership growth? The next section of this book presents each of the critical components for building your membership recruitment success story.

---

[34] Lisa Boylan, "Membership Success Stories Amid COVID-19."

PART TWO

HOW TO **RECRUIT** MEMBERS

CHAPTER FOUR

GETTING STARTED WITH MEMBERSHIP RECRUITMENT

Edwards Deming, the father of the quality control movement, popularized the methodology of PDSA (Plan-Do-Study-Act). It is a process for continuous improvement, and it has an application for how associations can go about getting started with membership recruitment.

In the **planning** phase of PDSA, an organization establishes objectives and processes. In the **do** phase, they initiate tests to gain feedback. The **study** phase is when data is gathered from these efforts and evaluated. Finally, the **act** phase is when the tested efforts deploy to start the cycle of information gathering and planning all over again.[35]

Unfortunately, some associations stumble in getting started with membership recruitment by either getting stuck in the planning phase or by thinking that they can skip these initial steps and go directly to the act phase without first laying a solid foundation.

Associations that get bogged down in the planning for recruitment may take so much time researching, analyzing, and discussing a potential program that marketing efforts are delayed or never happen. You might call this barrier the paralysis of analysis. Plans get held up with pushback like, "we cannot do that because…," "we have to check the bylaws," or "we need more research." To answer all these potential challenges and to document explanations, some organizations end up with a book-sized plan that takes them months or years to assemble. I will never forget a conversation with one membership director who was new to his job. Asked what his membership plan was, he responded that his executive director had given him the following marching orders: in year one, the goal was to learn about the organization; in year two, he was to create a membership

---

[35] "W. Edwards Deming."

marketing plan; in year three, he was to implement the plan. Not surprisingly, the executive director and the membership director were no longer with the association three years later as the membership counts continued to decline.

At the opposite extreme are associations that jump directly to the act phase by thinking that there is a "silver bullet" to membership recruitment without going through the process to accomplish their goal. An often-told example of this is an association board announcing a target for membership growth using a catchy phrase like "25,000 members by the year 2025," but not basing the objective on an understanding of what is required to accomplish the goal.

The board of one leading trade group, for example, set a goal to grow from 3,700 organization members to 4,500. A year later, they learned that instead of an increase, the association had decreased by 100 members. They asked me to consult with them to understand what happened. With minimal investigation, finding the answer to the problem was simple. They set a membership goal but did not allocate any budget to achieve the goal. The staff, therefore, did not plan any membership recruitment efforts. Everyone hoped or assumed that if their organization offered good value, potential members from around the globe would find them and join. It did not happen.

DEVELOPING A BALANCED RECRUITMENT PLAN

As it applies to association membership recruitment, the solution to avoid falling into either of these traps is creating a balanced approach with a rapid learning and continuous improvement mindset. I've found this continuous learning methodology to be akin to a "hurry up and wait" approach. The **hurry-up** is to quickly get an initial plan in place and launch a recruitment promotion in the marketplace to gather information. The **wait** is taking the time to listen to the market's response to inform plans going forward and then repeating the process.

One association shared with me that they had 100,000 non-member opt-in emails in their database from prospects who had registered on their website. They knew these prospects had shown an interest in the organization and would be eligible to join. All the ingredients were there to develop a simple plan to reach out to them and ask them to join. However, lacking research on what the message should be and on what services might appeal to these prospects, the association considered delaying their acquisition efforts. After learning about PDSA, they agreed to test an initial recruitment email effort to these individuals. The result was that the association realized a very positive return on their marketing investment. Through tracking which segments of the prospects decided to join, they also learned who was most likely to become a member of the association, and they were able to focus their future promotions on the highest-responding candidates.

Similarly, if we could go back in time to see the beginning of the process that resulted in the tremendous growth enjoyed by SHRM and ANA, described earlier in this book, we would see two organizations determined to grow membership following a step-by-step learning process. There was no master plan for SHRM to go from 45,000 members to 300,000 members or for ANA to go from 90,000 to 150,000 members. Instead, there was a plan to get started, and funding was made available to begin the recruitment promotions.

In our careers as association professionals, many of us have gone through a similar process of experimentation. As teenagers, few of us planned on a career in the association industry. My goal as a teenager was to play shortstop for the New York Yankees. Realizing that I was not going to be Derek Jeter, I turned to history in college and worked as a historian and writer for the National Park Service as my first professional job. When funding for the position dried up, I accepted the opportunity to try marketing with a Fortune 500 company by a hiring manager who liked to hire people who studied history. Ultimately, this led me to a fulfilling career working for a marketing agency. By getting started and learning as I went, I found my path forward.

There is no "perfect" in marketing, just better marketing.
Ideally, at each step of the recruitment process, something
is learned. Successful associations are learning organizations.

In the same way, a simple directional plan and some early efforts are the only essentials for launching a membership recruitment program. Implementing a hurry up and wait plan is essential because membership marketing is always an iterative process. There is no "perfect" in marketing, just better marketing. Ideally, at each step of the recruitment process, something is learned. Successful associations are learning organizations. As the renowned author, consultant, and professor, Philip Kotler observed, "They collect feedback from the marketplace, audit and evaluate results, and make corrections designed to improve their performance. Good marketing works by constantly monitoring its position in relation to its destination."[36]

---

[36] Kotler, *Kotler on Marketing*.

Of course, in establishing a plan for membership recruitment, an association should undoubtedly set a goal with a proposed outcome and completion date for what it wants to achieve. Taking time to address pressing problems is also necessary for a smooth-running program. However, the initial plan can be short and sweet and adjusted as you gather results. Kotler emphasized that an intricate plan is not necessary. He notes that "marketing plans should be simple and to the point. Some CEOs want only a one-page plan!"[37]

DETERMINING THE ECONOMIC
MODEL FOR RECRUITMENT

One crucial piece of the initial plan is to agree on an economic model to reach the association's new member goal, including setting aside the necessary budget and determining the projected lifetime value of a member. Many associations overestimate the return they will receive in acquiring a new member in the first year and underestimate the profitability of the lifetime value a member will deliver through renewals and purchases in subsequent years. As Sheri Jacobs warned in *The Art of Membership,* "Whether you have $10,000, $100,000, or $1 million to spend on your next recruitment campaign, your efforts should result in either a break-even scenario—recruiting enough new members to offset the cost of the campaign—or a small profit."[38]

Because of the cost to acquire and provide services to new members, it is vital to understand the economics of membership. Sustainable funding for a recruitment campaign will not make sense or receive organizational support unless the favorable economics of membership is understood. Two calculations underpin the economic model of recruitment.

The first is the calculation of the lifetime value of a member (detailed in Chapter 1). Unlike many products and services that have a onetime fee, membership is a continuity product. Like an annuity, members provide a predictable income stream. If a member remains with an association for ten years with a dues rate of $175 and non-dues purchases of $50 a year, the lifetime value for that member is $2,250. Determining this number for your association is critical. Seth Godin maintains that in marketing, "The most important thing to figure out is the lifetime value of a customer [or member]."[39] Lifetime value answers the question of why associations

---

[37] Kotler.

[38] Sheri Jacobs, *The Art of Membership.*

[39] Godin, *This Is Marketing.*

should spend dollars in membership recruitment even if, in the first year, the effort may not produce a positive return on investment.

MAXIMUM ACQUISITION COST

defines the theoretical maximum investment that can be made to acquire a member at a profit.

| TOTAL ANNUAL REVENUE PER MEMBER (DUES AND NONDUES) | TOTAL INCREMENTAL SERVICING COSTS PER MEMBER | AVERAGE TENURE |

However, the lifetime revenue stream produced by a member is only part of the equation. The second calculation looks at the costs associated with serving a member to determine an association's maximum acquisition cost (MAC). The MAC is the amount an association can theoretically spend to acquire a new member and still realize, over the long term, a profit from that member. To calculate the MAC, start with the lifetime value of a member and subtract the costs to service a typical individual or organizational member over their lifetime.

There are two basic options to determine what costs to include in this calculation: full servicing costs or incremental servicing costs. The full cost approach takes into consideration all the related expenses to service a member. This calculation would include a portion of the association's total salaries and benefits, office space, and operating expenses. On the other hand, the incremental cost approach takes into consideration just the additional costs that an association would incur to service one additional member. These costs might include printing and mailing an extra magazine and newsletter, sending marketing materials to promote the association's non-dues products, and sending out renewal notifications.

When first launching a recruitment program, associations benefit from using the incremental cost approach, which emphasizes the positive economic outcome of a new member. The logic for this decision is that, as effective recruitment efforts begin, the costs associated with an organization's infrastructure remain in place whether a new member comes on board or not. Fixed costs do not vary when an additional member joins. The incremental cost calculation considers this and only assigns expenses for the additional costs that will directly result from the new member. Ultimately, after substantial membership growth takes place, fixed costs will need to be considered as part of the equation because staffing levels, additional office space, and even a new headquarters building may be required to serve the burgeoning membership. The good news is that, with substantially more members, there will be revenue to help cover these costs. However, if you assign full costs in the early phase of the recruitment effort, the cost burden will strangle the program. I remember one CFO making the case that each $100 dues-paying member cost the association $300 when fully loaded with overhead. To highlight the problem with this way of thinking, tongue in cheek, I suggested that if this was indeed the case, they should ask all their members to leave to save money.

If, in our previous example, a member's lifetime value is $2,250 and the incremental servicing cost is $50 per year or $500 over the member's lifetime, the potential long-term profit or margin an association could achieve by adding a new member is $1,750. The question then comes down to how much of this projected revenue an association should spend to acquire a member. Many associations with a growing membership choose to invest at least the first year of dues in obtaining a new member. On top of this, if an association can manage the cash flow, a strong case can be made to spend even more to enable faster growth.

NEXT STEPS

The bottom line in getting started with membership recruitment is to take a continuous learning approach with a quick launch start-up recruitment plan using the knowledge and insight you have on hand and then deploying an initial effort to validate your assumptions. As author Tom Peters recommends, "Test fast, fail fast, adjust fast."[40]

In the upcoming chapters, we will take a deep dive into the four core areas of building a continuous learning recruitment program. These include identifying your target market, developing your membership offers, exploring the marketing channels to best reach prospects, and refining your message to present your association's value.

---

[40] "Tom Peters Quotes."

CHAPTER FIVE

THE TARGET MARKET –
WHO DO YOU WANT TO REACH?

Marco Polo was an Italian merchant, explorer, and writer known for his book, *Marvels of the World*, recording his travels to China and other countries in Asia in the eleventh and twelfth centuries. Today, he may be best remembered for the swimming pool game named after him.

In the game, one person chooses to be "it." She closes her eyes and, starting at one end of the pool, calls out "Marco." All the others playing the game in the pool must respond "Polo." The one who shouts "Marco" listens to the voices and tries to catch one of the players who yelled, "Polo." Players shout Marco as often as needed to try and locate and find a player. Once caught, that person then becomes the "it," and the game continues.

The Marco Polo game resembles one of the essential tasks associations need to undertake to be successful in membership recruitment: searching out prospective members in their target markets. At the start, you may have little or no idea of who to try to recruit as a member. The process, therefore, is to begin to explore all the options available to see where the best response will come from and develop an ongoing effort to test, track, and measure prospects in your marketing efforts.

Even if your message isn't perfect and your graphics leave something to be desired, reaching the right person with your invitation still has a higher chance of success compared to speaking to the wrong person, with all the other elements done to perfection.

Finding your target market is critical. Even if your message isn't perfect and your graphics leave something to be desired, reaching the right person with your invitation still has a higher chance of success compared to speaking to the wrong person, with all the other elements done to perfection. That is why, for years, marketers have followed the 40/40/20 rule. The rule maintains that 40 percent of the success of your marketing campaign depends on reaching the right audience. The second 40 percent of results depends on making the right offer. And the remaining 20 percent depends on all the other factors in the promotion.[41]

The importance of identifying your best prospects is still true today. In the book, *This Is Marketing*, Seth Godin says the foundation of your marketing is answering the question, "Who's it for? . . . Once you are clear on 'who's it for,' doors begin to open to you." [42] That is why every membership recruitment effort should start by asking the question, "who might be interested in joining?" and then searching out those potential members. In any given campaign, the results from the best group of prospects to the least responsive can vary by up to 1,000 percent. This chapter will outline who to target in your membership acquisition efforts and where to find these top prospects.

To start, when discussing target markets, we need to agree on the terms we will use. Marketers use a variety of names to designate who they are trying to reach. These terms range from personas to segments, to deciles, to audiences, to lists. All the terms are useful, but for consistency in this chapter, we will refer to these target groups as marketing lists. A list is a group of individuals definable by behavior, demographics, job titles, industry, or source. Designating these groups as a specific list allows for tracking and measurement of each part instead of the whole. An example of a list might be the non-member attendees of an organization's current annual meeting.

FINDING HOUSE MARKETING LISTS

For almost all associations, the top marketing lists are made up of prospects found in databases owned or accessible to an association. The starting place to find prospect names is in your central Association Management System (AMS). You may find other lists on your association's IT network or colleagues' hard drives. In some cases, your suppliers may hold additional records. We call all these records owned by you "house lists," and they represent a potential gold mine for recruitment marketing efforts.

In the search to find house lists, the starting place is to conduct a data census. Ideally, this review will identify the membership status (active or

---

[41] "What Is 40 40 20 Rule?"
[42] Godin, *This Is Marketing*.

non-member), the relationship the contact has with the association (i.e., attendee, book buyer), the count of people in that category, and the timeframe of the record's creation. Some of the lists you should find by conducting a census will include:

- Lapsed members
- Product buyers
- Website registrants
- Shopping cart abandons
- Conference and meeting attendees
- Membership inquirers

In addition to your association's database, another area to explore is lists held by your suppliers and partners. Hundreds of associations offer a newsletter produced through an independent publisher that may include non-member subscribers. An example of this would be SmartBrief. One education association, the Association for Supervision and Curriculum Development (ASCD), found that they had over 100,000 non-member subscribers to their SmartBrief newsletter who they could add to their recruitment efforts. [43] These lists include non-members who have demonstrated a proven interest in the association's field by subscribing. Another potential source of supplier lists are users of your private social network community. When they investigated it, the American Association of Pharmaceutical Scientists (AAPS) identified a list of 60,000 prospects with opt-in email addresses who received digests from their community.

To improve effectiveness, house lists you have identified can also be updated and enhanced. To be sure mailing records are accurate, run them through the USPS National Change of Address (NCOA) service, which has approximately 160 million permanent change-of-address records of individuals, families, and businesses who have alerted them of a change. If your lists are missing relevant data like the mailing or email addresses, or you need better demographic information like age, gender, or household income, you can have these data fields appended to your files. For company records, a wealth of firmographic data can be appended with information like industry, revenue, number of employees, and executives' titles.

[43] "Industries & Media Kits | SmartBrief."

FINDING OUTSIDE THIRD-PARTY
MARKETING LISTS

To grow membership, associations will need to reach out more broadly than house lists and identify outside lists to use in their recruitment efforts. Fortunately, there are many excellent opportunities to search for and find prospects from third-party lists and database providers.

To start finding outside lists, look at publishers and companies exhibiting at your conference and advertisers in your publications or website. If these entities are trying to reach your members, they well may have subscribers or customers who will also be prospects for your marketing efforts. Many of these organizations may rent their lists or agree to conduct a list exchange. For most associations, publications in their industry offer the best source of prospects since the records are typically well-maintained, and the subscribers have either qualified to receive the magazine or paid to receive it.

The next opportunity to locate outside lists includes reaching out to a professional list broker or doing the searches yourself with a media research website like NextMark.com. The type of file you will find through this process is generally rented on a one-time use basis. A list broker will recommend lists to you and place the order to secure the list. Just like a real estate broker, a list broker receives compensation from the list owner, so there are usually no additional charges to you beyond the list rental rate for this service.

On the other hand, using a website like NextMark provides a keyword tool that allows you to search thousands of commercially available lists on your own to find potential prospects. A search in NextMark will provide relevant data cards that include details about the list like the selects or segments available, whether the list offers email and telephone numbers along with mailing addresses, and the sources of the records.

When exploring outside lists, be aware that they fall into two broad categories: direct response lists and compiled lists. The differences are crucial in making your list decisions. Direct response lists include individuals who have responded to a marketing offer. These may consist of lists of magazine subscribers, catalog buyers, or even members of other associations. Effectively, names on a direct response list include another marketer's customer names. Because they are proven buyers, individuals on these lists are typically more responsive than those on compiled files. In contrast, compiled lists include names and addresses assembled from phone books, directories, or public records. The advantage of compiled lists is that they usually include a higher number of names and more detailed selection options, including demographics, job titles, telephone numbers, and company characteristics.

A final source of outside marketing lists are databases that can be leased for a specified time and repeatedly used instead of the customary one-time use with rented lists. These lists might include significant amounts of additional demographic or firmographic information. In the education marketplace, for example, Market Data Retrieval maintains thousands of data points on schools and colleges and the educators who work there. Lists can be rented for a single recruitment campaign or leased for an extended marketing program. Databases from other companies are available for most professions and industries.

BUILDING A LIST PYRAMID

As marketing lists are tested and tracked in your recruitment promotions, a hierarchy will emerge for the files that work best. One of the best ways to visually think through your target market is as a pyramid with the top layer indicating the best prospect lists and each lower layer displaying sequentially less-qualified lists of prospects. The bottom layer can represent entirely new markets that you are trying to reach for membership.

At the top of the pyramid, for most associations, will be their house lists. They will invariably produce better response rates than third-party lists. These prospects are aware of the association and, because the association owns these lists, there is no cost associated with renting them. Of the house lists, most associations will find that the very best performing lists are recently lapsed members. These are followed by lists of customers and attendees who paid full non-member prices for products or events and may be responsive to having the cost differential applied to their membership dues. Prospects that started the join process and then abandoned the website's shopping cart are also very likely to join when associations follow up with them immediately. Finally, the potentially large lists from a website's registered users, non-member subscribers, and private social community registrants are excellent candidates for email campaigns.

Outside marketing lists will invariably fall to the lower layers of your target market pyramid. Nevertheless, reaching these prospects is essential for significant growth. Through careful testing and tracking, you can assemble a portfolio of outside lists that lends breadth and depth to your recruitment promotions.

With a good understanding of the lists in your target market, you can explore the most effective channels to use based on where the list falls in your target market pyramid. I will explore the available marketing channels in chapter seven.

THE FUTURE OF MARKETING LISTS

For most associations, tracking the results of a recruitment effort by specific marketing lists is the appropriate and effective way to maximize results. However, as technology advances, more associations are moving beyond list-by-list analysis to data modeling, which essentially scores a single individual's likelihood to respond. Every data element attached to an individual is either a positive or negative predictor of joining. One method of scoring individuals is the RFM method, which stands for recency of purchase, the frequency of purchases, and the amount of spending on purchases. However, even more sophisticated data models will look at each piece of data associated with an individual's record because every data point correlates with a prospect's likelihood to join or not join. When you roll up these data points into a single score, a database can rank and array each person from most likely to least likely to respond. This scoring allows for maximum recruitment efficiency.

To succeed in the pool game of Marco Polo, you need to call out frequently and listen carefully to identify your target. Searching for the best prospects for your recruitment efforts is very similar. You need to wade through your house lists, locate and test outside lists, and enhance your data by keeping it clean and filling in what is missing. All the other pieces of membership recruitment are essential, but your top priority for a successful program will depend on finding your best prospective member targets.

Armed with this information, you can turn your attention to the second component of the continuous learning recruitment program: developing the most effective offers to convince these prospects to join your association.

CHAPTER SIX

THE MEMBERSHIP OFFER – WHAT DO YOU OFFER A PROSPECT?

Growing up, I remember watching *Let's Make a Deal* on TV. The television game show first aired in 1963, and for 30 years, Monty Hall served as the host. Contestants would dress up in crazy costumes and do wacky things to have the chance to make a deal. Amazingly, the show remains popular and continues to air on CBS today.

Your potential members probably are not prepared to go to great lengths, like the contestants on *Let's Make a Deal*, to get a special offer on membership, but let's face it: everyone loves to get a good deal on whatever they buy, and your potential members are no different.

Special offers to incentivize action are common when looking more broadly at just about any marketing effort. An incentive is used in selling magazine subscriptions, coupons are offered for groceries, and free phones are provided for contracting with wireless plans. Getting a good deal, for most consumers, is a top priority. One of the first questions anyone asks a friend who bought a new or used car is, "did you get a good deal?"

Special offers are employed not because companies enjoy giving away money but because they work to maximize profits both in the short and long term. People are motivated by a special offer to act now in making a buying decision. Marketing tests have documented that "offers can mean the difference between success and failure. Depending on the offer, differences in the response of 25, 50, or 100 percent and more are commonplace." [44] That is why, after identifying your target market, the second most powerful tool in membership recruitment is how you will

---

[44] Stone, *Successful Direct Marketing Methods.*

incentivize a prospect to join and make it easy for them to pay for their membership.

There are two questions to consider when designing a membership recruitment offer:

- What special incentives work best to encourage a prospect to act now and join?
- What payment options make the cost and commitment of joining easier and more manageable?

SPECIAL OFFERS

Today, a qualified member can likely join your association with a quick Google search and by providing some basic information and a credit card. Membership is available on a 24/7 basis. This access is an excellent service to those who know who you are and understand they need the value that you provide. However, as discussed previously, in marketing terms, association membership is a push product. It is sold and not necessarily sought after. Since it is continually available on your website, prospects likely feel no urgency to act. Because of this, incentives and special offers need to come into play. A special offer to join addresses the question of "why now?" and helps prospects to know that they are getting a better deal by acting right away instead of waiting.

A special offer to join addresses the question of "why now?" and helps prospects to know that they are getting a better deal by acting right away instead of waiting.

Special offers are most effective in membership recruitment when they are made available for a limited time with a specific expiration date. For a direct mail piece or print ad, the offer may be available for as long as several months. For email and digital marketing efforts, the timeframe can be much shorter, as with a one-day sale for Black Friday or Cyber Monday. In all cases, an offer requires a source code for the prospect to access the deal and for you to track and fulfill the promised incentive.

Providing an incentive to join has been a standard practice for associations over the years. As one survey respondent shared, "Any kind of promotions or discount has moved those on the fence to commit. Waive an enrollment fee, free gift with signup, limited time offer, [or] get in before the price goes up."

In the *Membership Marketing Benchmarking Report*, associations shared the top three recruitment offers they found to be most effective. The ranking included some of the following:

- Discount with conference registration – 58 percent
- First-year dues discount – 49 percent
- Additional free months of membership – 44 percent
- Product savings voucher – 35 percent
- Free trial or no-obligation membership – 30 percent
- Gifts or premiums – 25 percent
- Money-back guarantee – 22 percent
- Sweepstakes or contests – 13 percent [45]

Let's look more in-depth at how associations have used these offers and at the opportunities and challenges presented by each of them.

Discount with Conference Registration

Most associations with an annual meeting or conference have some type of offer to non-members who want to register. Some associations build a one-year membership into the non-member conference registration fee for an attendee. This deal means that every non-member attendee who registers consents to become a member and is automatically enrolled. Of course, an opt-out for membership is usually part of the registration process. Other groups follow up with the non-member either during or after the event. They offer a special deal to encourage them to make an active instead of a passive decision to join.

Both techniques have pluses and minuses. On the plus side, the attendee demonstrated an interest in the meeting's content and the financial resources to attend. These actions make the person a prime candidate to join. The hope is that the attendee will have a great experience and be enthusiastic about a membership relationship with the association.

Associations that enroll attendees as members when they register effectively achieve nearly a 100 percent response rate. Few marketing efforts can ever approach this level of response. Your marketing costs are your membership servicing costs that you are providing to the member over the year. Including membership with a meeting registration amounts to offering benefits as a marketing tool. If the member finds the services helpful and engaging, the likelihood of him or her renewing will be high. The challenge with this approach is that the member joined passively and, when renewal time comes around, typically only 10 to 20 percent of the members who joined by combining registration and membership will

---

[45] Rossell, Wasserman, and Kerr, "The Membership Marketing Benchmarking Report, 12th Edition."

renew. Still, very few recruitment efforts achieve a 10 percent paid response rate, so this offer makes sense with a reasonable conversion rate.

On the other hand, following up with the non-member attendee during or after the conference with a discount means those who make an active decision to convert will have a higher level of commitment. With this approach, the association also saves the cost of providing services to a member who may not value them. Since the attendee declined to seek out membership before registering for the conference, any follow-up recruitment efforts will only achieve a response rate typically realized with marketing efforts to other house lists. And the promotion will require dollars to be spent to reach these non-member attendees.

First Year Dues Discount

One of the most debated recruitment offers for first-year membership is a dues discount. The concern is that a member who joins with a lower dues rate will not be as loyal as one who comes to the association at the full price. However, respondents to the annual *Membership Marketing Benchmarking Report* almost always say that a new member discount represents one of the most effective recruitment incentives. The test results shared by many associations also confirm the effectiveness of offering a discount to get a member to join.

One of the most debated recruitment offers for first-year membership is a dues discount. The concern is that a member who joins with a lower dues rate will not be as loyal as one who comes to the association at a full price.

To validate the impact of a new member discount, one individual membership association conducted a test to 400,000 prospects by splitting their list evenly. One-half of the prospective members were offered membership at full price, and the second half received a $10 dues discount. All the other elements of the promotion were held constant. The test's outcome showed that the group receiving the discounted membership offer had a 40 percent higher response rate than the group offered the full dues rate. In addition to more members, the increase in response rate provided enough of a boost that the discount group also resulted in higher overall first-year total dues revenue.

The association then sought to answer the critical question of what the impact of the dues discount offer would have on the member retention rates over the long term. All members were required to renew at the full dues price. To find the answer, they tracked the members from the original recruitment test that joined at both the full dues amount and the discounted rate over two full renewal cycles. After two years, the analysis found that the group receiving the new member discount still outnumbered those initially joining at full price by 35 percent. The data showed that there was a slightly higher lapse rate from the discount group, but overall the association ended up with far more members and dues revenue. For them, the test validated the continued use of a new member dues discount as an incentive to join.

Will the use of a new member discount also work for a trade association? The National Business Aviation Association (NBAA) wanted to determine if membership could grow faster by trying a discount. To find out, they tested a substantially reduced price to prospective new member companies. They found offering the deep discount doubled the response rate compared to the usual return. When they looked at the continuance of members several years later, the discount group indeed had retained members at a lower rate. However, the association still had far more members overall from the discounted group than from the higher-priced promotions.

There is an essential qualification in using new member discounts: the level of an incentive should be tested because outcomes are not always intuitive. In some tests, associations have found that a 15 percent discount has often performed just as well as a 30 percent discount. Providing very steep discounts is not always required to have an attractive new member offer.

Additional Months Free

Associations that operate with a calendar year membership, where the membership year starts on the same month for all the members, find that offering additional months of membership at no added cost can be a compelling recruitment incentive. If, for example, the membership year starts on January 1, the organization has a dilemma on how to handle an individual or company who wants to join in October. Do you charge them for 15 months of membership? Or do you ask the prospect to pay for three months of membership and immediately turn around and send them a renewal notice?

The solution that many calendar year-based associations have come up with is to turn the dilemma into an opportunity to encourage membership. They simply invite prospects to join immediately and tell them that they'll receive the remainder of the current year at no additional cost when they pay for the upcoming year.

This offer is not limited to the calendar year membership organizations. One survey respondent from a trade association shared how she used this offer successfully, even though the organization used an anniversary membership model (twelve months of membership from the date a member joins). She said, "We ran a 'Cyber Week' deal the last week in November and secured 4% of our total new membership for the year in that week alone. The deal [was promoted] as 15 months of membership for the price of 12. The campaign was sent to all non-members in our database and increased awareness of our organization and the benefits and resources that we offer."

Product Voucher

Another compelling new member offer is providing a product voucher as an incentive to join. This offer effectively gives a new member a gift card to be used to attend a meeting or to purchase an association product for a limited timeframe after they join. Besides encouraging an upfront response, the added advantage of a voucher is that it incentivizes a new member to get engaged right away by using the products and services offered by the association. An engaged member is much more likely to renew.

A voucher can offer a substantial dollar amount to prospects. The association designates the products or services on which it can be redeemed. Some portion of the vouchers awarded to new members, often over 50 percent, will not be redeemed at all, and this further reduces the out-of-pocket expenses for the association.

One challenge to keep in mind with a voucher offer is that an association needs to determine how to fulfill it through the association's website. This process may require the voucher to be limited to specific products or services and fulfilled by entering a unique code on the site.

Free Trial or No-Obligation Membership

If you shop at Costco, you are familiar with the free samples that they share at the end of various aisles. These food items are intended not to provide shoppers with a free lunch, but to encourage the purchase of a product that customers may otherwise not have considered buying.

The same philosophy applies when offering samples of an association's benefits to prospective members. Various forms of free-trial and no-obligation membership have been used over the years to introduce prospects to join an association. The basic concept is to lower the risk for a potential member who may want to "try before they buy." An association provides this opportunity by sharing the membership products and services for a limited time of usually three to six months.

The opt-in free-trial method is perhaps the most common. This option features an initial promotion to prospects and asks them to accept a membership trial. Upon acceptance, the respondent receives membership for a specified period, and additional promotions go out requesting that he or she convert to a paid membership. Depending on the quality of the list, the initial response can be between three and five percent. The final conversion can be as high as 30 percent of those who accepted the trial membership.

A variation of the free trial is the no-obligation membership. With this method, the association also gives a prospective member the chance to sample membership benefits. However, there is a significant difference. When a prospect agrees to the no-obligation trial, he or she also agrees to allow the organization to invoice them for the membership with the stipulation that the respondent has the choice to pay the invoice to continue the membership or write "cancel" on the invoice to end the trial. Those who cancel can keep the benefits that they have received to that point and owe nothing.

Getting permission upfront from a prospective member to invoice them with the no-obligation offer can dramatically increase the final paid rate, especially if potential members can submit the invoice for payment to their company. Because you can send an invoice from a no-obligation offer, the paid conversion rate is much higher compared to the more traditional free-trial offer.

Both free-trial and no-obligation offers will initially almost always perform better than pay-now offers. The key to the ultimate result is managing a robust conversion series that asks for payment and providing valuable member benefits that encourage continuance. If the food you sample at Costco tastes delicious, you may very well buy it. In the same way, these offers usually work best with organizations that have a rich serving of valuable and tangible benefits to share with members to convince them to continue.

Money-Back Guarantee

In a review of many associations' join pages, it is surprising how few highlight a money-back satisfaction guarantee. For most direct marketing companies and retailers, a guarantee or return policy is almost automatic. Associations who offer a guarantee have an easier time implementing it than most companies because their only obligation is to refund the dues payment. Unlike commercial enterprises, associations do not incur costs of shipping, re-stocking, or re-selling products.

The purpose of a money-back guarantee is to lower the perceived risk of joining. It highlights that the association is confident that membership provides exceptional value. The best guarantee offers an unconditional full refund at any time during the membership year if a member's expectations go unmet. For a program to get the maximum benefit from a guarantee, prominently display it on the join page of the website and promotional pieces.

When associations provide a membership satisfaction guarantee, there is seldom a high level of redemption. It is more likely that, if members do not like what they receive, they simply do not renew. For those who do request a refund, it allows the association to address the concern or at least learn from the dissatisfied member and make improvements.

Gift or Premium

Offering a gift or premium as an incentive to join comes with some complexity. First, compared to a discount or additional months of membership, there is time and expense involved in creating and fulfilling the premium. Secondly, there is a wide variance in the effectiveness of these promotions depending on the gift you select. It is wise to test different gift options to see what appeals to prospective members.

However, identifying the right premium can be highly successful. The American Intellectual Property Law Association (AIPLA) uses its Economic Survey, which is produced every other year, as an incentive for new members to join. The survey provides data on the annual incomes for intellectual property attorneys and patent agents. It examines other vital topics, including individual billing rates and typical charges for intellectual property legal services.[46] This must-have information speaks to both a prospect's self-interest (am I being paid appropriately?) and to the firm's self-interest (are we billing appropriately?). The result is that the offer drives reliable response rates year after year.

A recruitment gift does not always have to be a sample of a product usually provided by the association. The American Association for the Advancement of Science (AAAS) tapped into scientists' identity by offering T-shirts as an incentive to join that feature science-related images and messages.

One mistake that is sometimes made by associations in selecting a gift is to move unused inventory. For example, an association might offer an overstocked book as an incentive to join, but if the book is not of interest to a portion of prospective members, it will decrease response rates.

---

[46] "Report of the Economic Survey."

Sweepstakes or Contests

Sweepstakes are used by companies ranging from Publishers Clearing House to the QVC shopping channel to McDonald's with their Monopoly contest. The purpose is to increase visibility, interaction, and, ultimately, sales. For membership recruitment, sweepstakes will typically work best for associations with lower-priced dues when a purchase is more of an impulse buy like a magazine-based membership.

Probably the most eye-catching sweepstakes program by an association is run by the Aircraft Owners and Pilots Association (AOPA). AOPA uses sweepstakes to encourage new members to join, renew, and purchase their products and services. Amazingly, each year the AOPA sweepstakes awards a fully refurbished airplane with the latest safety equipment along with a hundred additional prizes. The process of restoring the aircraft is highlighted month after month in the AOPA magazine. When they award the plane each year, it becomes a media event in the aviation field.

You do not need to have a sweepstake as big as giving away an airplane like AOPA to have success. The Northern California Golf Association, for example, runs annual sweepstakes for members to join or renew, offering hundreds of prizes ranging from the grand prize of a round of golf for two at the Pebble Beach Golf Links to a dozen Titleist Pro V1 golf balls. However, whatever your contest, it is critically important to consider the stringent Federal Trade Commission (FTC) rules and local laws that apply to any sweepstakes. For example, AOPA makes it clear that "No purchase or contribution [is] necessary to enter or win. A purchase or contribution will not improve your chances of winning." [47] Without the proper notifications, a contest can pose substantial legal challenges for an organization.

---

[47] "The AOPA Sweepstakes."

MEMBERSHIP PAYMENT OPTIONS

In addition to incentivizing members to join with special offers, you also want to make it easy for them to join and ultimately to renew. Associations can accomplish this by providing potential members with favorable payment options.

Installment Dues Payments

One of the most effective options to make membership payments more affordable is offering installment dues payments.

If you think about it, our society has moved to a month-by-month financial lifestyle. Your mobile phone, internet, and car payments are divided up and paid for every month. Our likelihood of purchasing any of these products would diminish if we were required to pay in advance. Just multiply your monthly mobile phone bill by twelve to see what your out-of-pocket expense would be if you had to pay it up front.

Today more membership associations are joining this trend and making installment dues payments an option for members. The *Membership Marketing Benchmarking Report* shows that fully 29 percent of individual associations and 32 percent of trade associations say they offer a monthly or quarterly installment option.

To see if an installment option would work to increase the response for membership recruitment, the American Occupational Therapy Association (AOTA) conducted a marketing test. Their prospect base was split 50/50, with 37,000 prospects getting the standard control $225 offer to join and the other 37,000 candidates receiving the additional option of paying the full price or a monthly automatic credit card installment of $18.75 a month. The results were impressive. The control package with the one-time payment option generated 436 new members for a 1.17 percent response rate. However, the test package with the installment option produced 657 members for a 1.77 percent response rate. Many more prospects were more willing to join if they had the opportunity to pay monthly.

Additionally, over time AOTA looked at how members who selected the monthly installment option renewed compared to members who paid up front. Again, the results supported the installment offer. The on-time renewal rate for those members not on the installment plan was 55 percent. The on-time renewal rate for members signed up for the installment plan was 82 percent. The non-installment member rate ultimately reached 70 percent after including late renewal payments. Yet, even when adding late responses, the twelve-point lift in renewals was a remarkable validation of making a monthly payment option available.[48]

Annual Automatic Credit Card Payment

Another payment method that is becoming commonplace today is an annual automatic credit card payment or Electronic Funds Transfer (EFT) from a checking account. Corporate giants—from Costco to Microsoft to Amazon—offer this option, as well as many associations. According to survey data, automatic payments are made available by 37 percent of individual membership associations.

Some associations even have this payment method as the default for a member to join the association in their electronic membership category. The rationale is that this inexpensive membership category is paperless and does not generate income to cover the costs of sending out renewal notices.

The reason the automatic payment option is so popular is simple. If you can get a new member to agree to this option when they initially join, the renewal rate in the next year will typically be at least a full 10 points above those not in the program. To encourage members to sign up for the program, Costco currently offers members a $20 gift card. Some associations will also provide an incentive for members to select this option. The Aircraft Owners and Pilots Association provides a $4 dues discount to encourage members to enroll in the automatic annual credit card payment program.

Legally there are specific requirements for an association to offer automatic credit card billing. You must disclose the terms of the program and obtain the member's consent to participate. Members also need to have the ability to cancel and receive notification of changes to the terms of service like a dues increase.[49] Putting in place this option has become more straightforward as most Association Management Systems (AMS) have the capability of running this transaction.

Longer-Term Membership

A third payment method to review is offering potential members a longer-term membership option. This option includes multi-year and lifetime membership. At first glance, these would not seem to be very appealing options in membership recruitment, as prospects may view them as too expensive or risky—like purchasing the giant-size version of a product at the grocery store that you have never tried before. Still, the

---

[48] "Auto-Renewal and Monthly Payments."

[49] "Whiteford Taylor Preston, LLP | Automatic Renewal of Membership Dues and Recurring Credit Card Payment Laws."

benchmarking data show that 22 percent of associations offer multi-year memberships and 15 percent offer life memberships.

The attraction for these membership options for a prospective member is significant savings. If potential members know that they are in a profession that they spent years preparing to enter, and if they have the funds, it makes sense to pocket the savings. My son, when he graduated from college, qualified for membership in the Phi Kappa Phi honor society. He could pay $65 annually, $90 for two years, or $300 for life. At his age, the life option seemed to make sense to maintain membership and to be able to continue to include the honor on his profile and resume.

Group Payment

Another recruitment program that makes joining and renewing easier, especially for a company, is offering a group membership where a firm pays the dues for individual members on a single annual invoice. The Public Relations Society of America, Inc. (PRSA), for example, allows a group of members to join with a single, combined annual payment. With group membership, a company does not have to track numerous individual payments and can save money with a group discount. Membership in the PRSA group is transferable to a new employee who joins the company, and the larger the group, the less expensive the dues are per member.[50]

One benchmarking survey respondent added, "Group membership has been very effective in capturing a full team of professionals in an organization rather than just managers. This has led to more training and conference attendance."

A big success story with group membership is the Society of Cable Telecommunications Engineers (SCTE). SCTE wanted to keep their status as an individual membership association but also wanted to engage their members' employers. The solution was to create a group membership partner program. The program offered companies discounts on dues and training when they enrolled a larger portion of their employees as SCTE members. The result was that "in less than two years, SCTE's individual membership has increased from 14,000 to more than 20,000 as a result of the partner program, and its training revenue has doubled."[51]

---

[50] "Group Membership."
[51] "Membership Memo."

NEXT STEPS

One dictionary definition of inertia is "a tendency to do nothing or to remain unchanged." Ultimately, association recruitment efforts are about overcoming potential members' inertia. When it comes to promoting your membership, a push is needed to help your prospects move from indecision to giving the association a try. As I hope you gathered from this chapter, there are many options to help potential members answer the question "why now?" and to support them and their company to make the investment as easy as possible.

In the next chapter, we will bring together the elements of targeting your audience and your new member offers with a view of the channels that are available to reach out to your prospects.

CHAPTER SEVEN

THE MARKETING CHANNELS – HOW DO YOU REACH A PROSPECT?

When you look at the developments in mass communication, you see change coming at an accelerating pace. Almost 500 years elapsed between China's first use of moveable type printed on paper to the Guttenberg printing press. In 1844, three hundred years later, the telegraph was introduced. Next came the telephone in 1876, the radio in 1896, and the television in 1927. With the introduction of the personal computer and the internet, the pace of change has been even more rapid. The use of email came into play in 1972, the first cell phone in 1973, texting in 1992, smartphones in 2001, Facebook and LinkedIn in 2003, and the first tweet transmission came in 2006.[52] Today, all these will move faster with the introduction of 5G networks running 10 to 20 times faster than 4G.

Over the years, almost all these communication developments have impacted marketing. Many principles of marketing do not change, such as the importance of focusing on target markets, presenting offers, and the underlying economics of membership, but how we reach a prospective member will continue to evolve. It may be hard for younger readers to believe. Still, just 30 years ago, the marketing mix available today—websites, social media, email, digital ads, and texting—did not exist.

Instead of each marketing channel working independently,
successful membership recruitment now requires each
marketing channel to work in unison through coordinated
timing, offers, branding, and messages.

---

[52] "The History of Communication Technology."

Because of these changes and with the breadth and depth of new marketing tools now available, it makes sense to rethink how we apply them. Over the last few decades, membership recruitment has moved from a multichannel approach, where perhaps a mailing was sent out or a phone call was made to invite someone to join, to an omnichannel methodology. Instead of each marketing channel working independently, successful membership recruitment now requires each marketing channel to work in unison through coordinated timing, offers, branding, and messages.

The good news is that used correctly, this coordination of marketing channels produces better results and, for many associations, has accelerated their membership growth. Research has shown that "omnichannel marketing has been proven to drive results. A survey by International Data Corporation found that omnichannel buyers typically achieve a 30 percent higher lifetime value than single-channel buyers."[53] One trade association, The National Business Aviation Association (NBAA), is an example of how the use of omnichannel marketing in its membership recruitment efforts has helped the association to nearly double its membership.

A TRADE ASSOCIATION STORY

In 2006, the business aviation industry faced legislative and regulatory changes that would have imposed substantial user fees and restrictions on their access to airports. The industry turned to NBAA for help to meet these threats. One of the first steps that NBAA leadership took to increase the effectiveness of the association's voice was to grow membership to support the association's advocacy efforts. NBAA set an ambitious long-term goal to grow its membership by actively recruiting more companies in the aviation industry. The results were that, after a little more than a decade, the number of member companies had increased by 83 percent.

To achieve this growth, NBAA moved its recruitment efforts over time to an omnichannel approach using a full portfolio of channels including direct mail, email, content marketing, digital ads, telemarketing, and personal sales outreach.

One of the critical decisions by NBAA was to focus on direct mail to reach a broad range of individuals who could influence companies' deliberations regarding membership in the association. The process that a company goes through to join an association is different from that of an individual. Hence, trade associations need to speak to multiple staff

---

[53] Kotler, Kartajaya, and Setiawan, *Marketing 4.0.*

members of a company to build a consensus to join and identify a champion who will push the decision forward. NBAA identified direct mail lists that contained contacts across the spectrum of those who might be involved in a decision to join, including pilots, operations, maintenance, and management staff. They also found that coordinating the timing and messages of their direct mail with email produced even better results.

NBAA was also one of the early association users of online digital ads for membership recruitment. Targeted digital ads on Facebook and LinkedIn, along with Google search engine marketing (SEM), helped to both attract leads through content marketing for the sales team and to help them sell membership directly. Content marketing helped to add new opt-in records to the prospect database by making relevant whitepapers available like "Ten Critical Strategies for Long-term Fuel Savings." To access the content, respondents needed to provide their contact information and consent to opt-in before receiving additional communications from NBAA. To reach those members whose membership lapsed, a telemarketing supplier successfully reached out to contacts to remind them that their membership was no longer in force and to ask them to reinstate.

One final component of the recruitment efforts was adding a dedicated salesperson to the team to help close sales with prospective member companies. Her outreach focused on top companies that had recently sent an attendee to an event or had downloaded a content offer. Prospects who had started to complete an online membership application and abandoned their cart also received immediate follow-up. Having a dedicated person to find the decision-maker in a company and close the deal was especially useful for this trade group.

As a result of following this omnichannel approach, NBAA membership grew from 6,000 to 11,000 companies[54], and they were able to very effectively make their case before Congress in support of their members' businesses. Membership recruitment helped NBAA fulfill its mission.

EXPLORING RECRUITMENT MARKETING CHANNELS

For associations, many marketing channels have proven to be especially useful for membership recruitment. Let's explore these channels and the opportunities and challenges associated with each of them.

---

[54] "NBAA Reaches 11,000-Member Mark."

Email

The annual *Membership Marketing Benchmarking Report* highlights email as the second most effective recruitment channel behind word of mouth. The prominence of email makes sense. Email is inexpensive, quick to deploy, provides links directly to the association's website, and is highly trackable and measurable. For example, most email systems allow for an A/B test of a limited portion of the email to determine which version has a higher open rate or click-through rate. This option is known as 10/10/80 testing. It offers almost instant feedback to optimize the effectiveness of the promotion by sending 10 percent of the list one version of the email and a second 10 percent the test version. The winner then goes to the remaining 80 percent of the list.

Email deployed by associations also shows very favorable levels of engagement. Higher Logic's *Association Email Marketing Benchmark Report* says the average email metrics for associations include a 98.3 percent delivery rate, a 35.6 percent open rate, and a 15.6 percent click rate.[55]

However, some associations who rely too heavily on email to acquire new members are limiting their growth potential because the channel comes with some notable limitations. Since the level of relationship with non-members is much lower than with a member who has paid to receive communications from an association, not surprisingly, recruitment emails have a comparatively lower open rate. The overuse of this channel can ultimately lead to diminished response rates.

Besides lower open rates and overuse, the other challenge with using email to acquire members is its limited exposure to potential audiences. Most associations can only email prospects in their database. This limitation means that, over time, they are "preaching to the choir" and not expanding their market reach. Unless there is a concerted effort to add new contacts, the results of email recruitment campaigns will eventually fade.

One alternative for an association wanting to reach out beyond its database is to rent email lists from a third party. These email lists can be rented typically for a one-time usage but will cost up to $350 per thousand emails sent. Additionally, the company that manages the email list handles the deployment. So, removing current members for a recruitment effort will require associations to share their existing membership file with the sender or risk having members receive the solicitation.

The best solution for connecting with prospective members beyond those in your database is adding other channels into your marketing mix

---

55 "HigherLogic_Report_Association Email Marketing Benchmark Report 2017.Pdf."

that offer a broader reach. These channels include direct mail and digital advertising.

Direct Mail

Over the years, direct mail has proven to be the workhorse of membership recruitment. The *Membership Marketing Benchmarking Report* highlights that, especially for individual membership associations, direct mail remains one of the most effective tactics to get new members.

The strengths of direct mail are threefold. First, there is an abundance of highly targeted lists in almost any field or industry with thousands of names on them that offer an association with a significant volume of prospective members. Secondly, direct mail has a longer shelf life than digital channels. Prospects tend to hold onto a direct mail piece, so new members may sign up months after receiving the mailing. Finally, direct mail appears to be able to connect with prospects in ways that digital communications do not. One study conducted for the Center for Experimental Consumer Psychology at Bangor University found that "the physicality of print creates an emotional connection for those who handle it. Ink on paper makes a deeper impression in the brain than something nonphysical like a digital message."[56]

Direct mail even continues to be compelling with younger prospects and members. In Personify, Inc.'s report, *Young Members 2.0*, over 1,000 Millennials and Generation Z association members shared their opinions. The research found that direct mail was still effective in engaging younger members. Many young members reported that they receive direct mail from their organization, and 76 percent said it was either very or somewhat effective.[57] Anecdotally, I remember one millennial who works for a client telling me that she rarely gets mail, so it is exciting to find something in her mailbox.

Despite these positive attributes, some associations have given up on mail for both recruitment and, in some cases, renewals. And there are some legitimate challenges in managing a successful direct mail program.

The biggest challenges are cost and time. With postage and paper prices increasing, the cost to acquire a member with direct mail has risen over the past decade. Today, for direct mail to be cost-effective, it needs to be even more highly targeted to the best prospects. Associations that in the past could mail significant volumes and receive a positive ROI may find the economics have changed, requiring them to reduce quantities by as much as 50 percent. Mail also takes time to print and send. A direct mail effort sometimes takes several months to create and deploy, so it does not

[56] Bly, *The Direct Mail Revolution.*
[57] "Young Members 2.0."

provide the instant gratification found in email campaigns. Nevertheless, many of the associations highlighted in this book have achieved significant membership growth using direct mail for recruitment and depend on it to renew their members. For most associations, direct mail should hold a central place in an omnichannel marketing mix.

Paid Online Digital Marketing

Paid digital advertising is the fastest growing and one of the most cost-effective marketing channels available for recruiting members. Benchmarking research highlighted that 15 percent of individual membership associations now say that digital ads are one of their most effective recruitment channels.[58]   Digital ads primarily include paid advertising on Facebook, Google, AdRoll, and LinkedIn, along with ads purchased on other websites and online publications.

Paid digital advertising is the fastest growing and one of the most cost-effective marketing channels available for recruiting members.

Many benefits make digital ads advantageous for membership recruitment. These include:

- Awareness – More prospects will see your ads than will click on them, but with many platforms, you pay for clicks and not impressions.
- Coverage – Digital advertising gives you access to every corner of the world where there is an internet connection.
- Flexibility – With digital ads, you can adjust and allocate funds daily to maximize response.
- Speed – You can have a digital advertising program operational and producing responses in a day.
- Measurement – You can determine impressions, clicks, and—with proper tracking—the number of members who join from each ad.

Two of the methods used effectively for membership recruitment with digital ads are creating custom audiences and lookalike audiences. Custom audiences work by uploading and matching a list of prospects to a platform like Facebook. The people on your uploaded list that match Facebook's users see your membership recruitment ads. Lookalike audiences work in reverse. In this case, you upload your current members to Facebook, and Facebook uses their algorithms to identify and show ads to the people who resemble your members.

---

[58] Rossell, Wasserman, and Kerr, "The Membership Marketing Benchmarking Report, 12th Edition."

In an interview with ASAE's *Associations Now*, the director of membership for the American Nurses Association shared how successful using Facebook had been with direct join appeals, and especially implementing a "lookalike" campaign. The ads targeted Facebook users who 'looked' like ANA members. The ads highlighted the value of the low monthly membership option for ANA of $15 per month. The result of the campaign was that it brought in nearly 650 new members in six months.[59] Facebook also offers additional targeting options beyond audience matching, including consumer demographics, interests, behavior, and geographic location.

Along with custom and lookalike audiences, LinkedIn provides exceptional professional and industry targeting options that can be very helpful to associations. With LinkedIn, you can target prospects based on:

- Demographics, including age, gender, and location;
- Jobs, including titles, function, skills, and years worked;
- Experience, including education level, degrees, and field of study;
- Interests, including LinkedIn groups;
- Company, including industry and size.

Associations are also using other digital opportunities successfully, like search engine marketing (SEM), YouTube, Geofencing (targeting prospects based on their physical location, building, or address), and search engine optimization (SEO). Also, one study of young association Millennials and Generation Z members highlighted that Instagram was a primary online source where they connected with their association.[60]

One additional tool that is an important starting place for associations interested in digital marketing is retargeting.

Retargeting

In most cases, any marketing efforts that you do will drive members and customers to your website to act. However, once prospects come to your website, many do not complete their transaction on the first visit. For example, very often, potential attendees visit an association's website to find out the date, location, or cost of a conference. These prospects rarely register right away. They may need to check their calendar, the cost of flights, or get budget approval to attend.

The same is true for new members deciding to join. They may need company approval for the purchase, or they may want to do some additional research. One organization with a high dues rate reported that they had nearly 10,000 shopping cart abandons on their membership application form each year.

---

[59] "Member Acquisition."
[60] "Young Members 2.0."

Because an organization's website is core to the join process, and because many prospective members do not buy on their first visit, adding retargeting (also known as remarketing) to a website is a necessity. A retargeting program involves adding code to specific pages of your website that places "cookies" on the computer of your site's visitors and then shows them relevant ads when they leave your site, reminding them to return. The primary providers of retargeting advertising are Google, AdRoll, and Facebook. Google and AdRoll show retargeting ads on a wide range of websites that accept ads. Facebook retargeting ads appear within Facebook applications.

Of all the digital advertising opportunities, retargeting will produce members at the lowest cost because a prospect has already shown interest by visiting the association's website. As one benchmarking respondent shared, "Digital AdRoll marketing has been a great new endeavor." Adding retargeting to your website is a fundamental step of an omnichannel marketing effort.

Telemarketing

There are challenges to running an effective telemarketing program. With Caller ID and voicemail, getting through to a prospective member on the phone has become more difficult. Moreover, when calls do get through, they can be considered a nuisance by the person that you reach.

However, telemarketing also provides associations with some unique advantages when used for membership recruitment. When you run a telemarketing program, you get immediate feedback and results, so you can quickly test offers and messages. You will know in a day or two of calling if the offer is working or you need to rework your script. It is also highly measurable and trackable. Each day you can calculate your ROI to see if the program is achieving your goal. If it is not producing the desired results, it can be turned off quickly after making only a portion of the calls. Finally, unlike other marketing channels that offer only one-way communication, telemarketing is a one-on-one interactive channel. Questions from a prospective member or sales objections can be addressed right away by a well-trained caller.

Telemarketing is especially productive for reaching highly qualified prospects such as lapsed members or recent customers. Often a call is received with gratitude by lapsed members who may have forgotten to renew or by customers who did not get a member discount for something that they purchased from you. For trade associations with higher dues levels, telemarketing can be a valuable tool to reach a significant number of companies with the goal of scheduling follow-up appointments to close a sale.

Many organizations use a telemarketing vendor to do their calling. The vendor has predictive dialing systems that allow for maximum efficiency, and they have experienced callers. Often, they also provide you with the ability to listen in on calls to evaluate their performance and make adjustments. Some trade groups and smaller membership associations use their staff or member volunteers for low volumes of calling. These calls can be particularly worthwhile because they can leverage a relationship that may exist between the volunteer and the prospective member.

Personal Sales and Account-Based Marketing

One of the newer terms used to describe the personal sales process is Account-Based Marketing (ABM), which is essentially a highly targeted personal sales approach to qualified individuals or companies. The concept has come into prominence as organizations have moved from a "spray and pray" sales philosophy to instead collecting data about a prospect and building a strategy around the integration of sales and marketing efforts. ABM is sales efforts on steroids.

In a membership recruitment context, the synergy offered by Account-Based Marketing is very appropriate for business-to-business membership marketing efforts, particularly for trade associations with high dues-paying members. The *Membership Marketing Benchmarking Report* highlights that fully 46 percent of trade associations count personal sales outreach as one of their most effective recruitment options. Account-Based Marketing focuses on establishing and deepening engagement when the purchasing decision involves a lengthy sales cycle and multiple decision-makers.

Predictably, a company is not typically going to decide to join a membership organization for thousands of dollars in dues payments based on a one-time sales contact. Instead, the regular communications, relationship development, and prospect knowledge built into Account-Based Marketing programs empower this process.

Here is how Account-Based Marketing works for membership recruitment. The first step is to identify prospects that fit into the membership profile and capture them in a database. The records for these companies or institutions can be leased from third party data compilers. At this point, these organizations may have little or no awareness or even an interest in membership. A process is needed to turn these generic listings in the database into warm prospects using both new and classic marketing efforts. This phase of the sales process is where the integration of sales and marketing is critical.

Account-Based Marketing uses direct mail and emails to build awareness and set up appointments to begin the conversation between the association's representative and the prospective company. Based on these appointments, the association's representative continues the discussion by providing sample content or industry data to show how the association can provide value.

As these interactions take place, the sales team catalogs the prospect's needs and decision process in the sales database. Additional contacts who might participate in a company's decision to join can also be added. This intelligence builds a profile of the decision maker's needs and decision process to help close the sale successfully.

Member-Get-A-Member Programs

As long as there have been membership organizations, there have been member-get-a-member (MGM) programs. These programs make a lot of sense because your members are likely to be in contact with potential members who share the same interests and needs as they do. Consistently, over the years, respondents to the *Membership Marketing Benchmarking Report* say that "word of mouth" referrals are the most valuable membership recruitment channel for associations. This experience is not only valid for associations, but virtually any business also depends on recommendations from customers for their success.

Most MGM programs include some type of incentive to encourage members to participate. These programs offer gifts or financial incentives, a contest, or recognition before members' peers in the association.

There are three main MGM methods that associations have used successfully to recruit new members. The first method is a "free trial" approach. Current members might receive a coupon that they can share with colleagues, offering a six-month free trial to try out the association. The strength of this program is that a member does not need to sell anything. They simply ask a friend to sample something that they value and use themselves.

A second MGM method is going to members and requesting them to provide the contact information for potential members. IEEE uses this method by directing members to an online form where they can submit their colleague's contact information. IEEE then follows up with an email invitation sent on the member's behalf to the recommended prospect. When the person referred joins, the member earns a financial reward to use toward IEEE dues or the purchase of books and publications.[61] The IEEE provides $15 for each new member recruited.

---

[61] "IEEE Member Referral Form | IEEE Forms."

A third approach run by a trade association is an actual member-to-member sales effort. This MGM program empowers members with the authority to offer a dues discount to a company that they recruit. For example, they can provide a 20 percent discount on first-year dues to any firm they recruit.

MGM programs can be a productive contributor to an omnichannel recruitment program. Whatever MGM method you put in place, the driver of success will be identifying, supporting, and encouraging the evangelists in your membership. These committed members are the key to a successful effort.

Other Channels

One of the challenges of omnichannel marketing approaches is spreading an association focus too broadly. Not every channel will rank as highly as another. An association should focus most of its time and resources on the most productive channels, and traditionally the most productive recruitment options are those highlighted here. Nevertheless, other methods to consider are exhibiting at your and other associations' conferences; using print advertisements, especially in your association's publication; texting; and employing chapter recruitment support programs. In the years to come, new channels will undoubtedly become available to enhance membership recruitment efforts.

TARGET MARKETS BY CHANNEL

In our chapter on target markets, I introduced the pyramid concept. Each layer of the pyramid segmented the prospective members. The most-likely-to-respond prospects appeared at the top and the less likely to respond candidates at sequentially lower levels. When evaluating what marketing channels to use in membership recruitment, the pyramid is also a helpful visual illustration. In your marketing campaigns, spending should flow down the pyramid from the top layer to the bottom. This approach ensures that the most expensive marketing channels should focus on top prospects. At the highest levels of the pyramid, most associations can afford to use telemarketing efforts and direct mail along with less expensive channels like email and digital ads to reach this high-priority segment. Trade associations and organizations with costly dues can also add personal sales outreaches for this top segment.

THE TARGET MARKETING PYRAMID

Former Members

Customers

Inquirers

Members of like associations

Subscribers

Directories

In the middle layers of the pyramid, it is unlikely that sales calls and telemarketing will be cost-effective. Reach these prospects with more affordable efforts like direct mail, email, and digital ads. At the bottom of the pyramid, where the least likely candidates to join sit, the only channels that may be cost-effective for recruiting new members may be sending out emails and showing these prospects online ads.

Even though your marketing funds and efforts are focused on the top target markets, the goal for substantial membership growth is always to go as deeply as possible in your market and, when appropriate, to test brand new markets. The pyramid is not meant to be limiting but used to maintain your focus. In chapter nine, we will look at how to test, track, and analyze marketing results to help efficiently reach as many prospects as possible for each dollar you have available.

LEGAL AND ETHICAL ISSUES

With any discussion of using marketing channels, one critical consideration is following ethical and legal privacy rules. With email in the United States, legislation passed in 2003—Controlling the Assault of Non-Solicited Pornography and Marketing Act (CAN-SPAM)—sets the requirements for those who send unsolicited commercial emails. The Act bans false or misleading information and requires that unsolicited email be identified as advertising along with providing a method for opting out of receiving future emails.[62]

Canada's Anti-Spam Legislation (CASL) requires senders to obtain consent, provide identification information, and provide an unsubscribe mechanism.[63] When it comes to data privacy, many organizations are following the EU General Data Protection Regulation (GDPR) in the United States, as well as where it is required.[64]

For telemarketing, although some non-profit entities are exempt, it is good practice to follow the rules of the Federal Trade Commission's Telemarketing Sales Rule (TSR). This rule allows people to register their phone number on the Do Not Call Registry to opt-out of commercial phone calls.[65]

Finally, there is also a non-legal, but a strongly recommended ethical practice that you should consider with your direct mail marketing: suppressing individuals from your mailings who have added their address to the DMA Choice mail preference service. Consumers on the list have asked not to receive mail solicitations.[66]

---

[62] "Controlling the Assault of Non-Solicited Pornography and Marketing Act of 2003 (CAN-SPAM Act)."
[63] Government of Canada, "Canada's Anti-Spam Legislation."
[64] "EUGDPR – Information Portal."
[65] "The Telemarketing Sales Rule."
[66] "DMAChoice - Do Not Mail List - Direct Mail Preference Service."

CHAPTER EIGHT

THE MARKETING MESSAGE –
WHY SHOULD A PROSPECT JOIN?

Despite managing an aggressive membership marketing program, the American Society for Quality (ASQ) found that membership had plateaued. ASQ had a rich portfolio of products and services to offer members, including the award-winning *Quality Progress* magazine, eighteen unique certifications, local section memberships, technical divisions, online and onsite training options, and a private social network. So, why wasn't membership growing?

ASQ believed that a missing element was finding a way to consolidate these benefits under a unifying and compelling message to help attract members. Some will call this unifying message an "elevator speech" to quickly and clearly define the benefit of membership. Another useful term used by marketers is a unique selling proposition (USP). The term was introduced by ad executive Rosser Reeves, who maintained that the USP should describe "the number-one factor that makes your product, service, or offer different and better than all others. When you highlight one key point—your USP—and drive it home again and again, you get your message across, and it sticks in the reader's mind."[67]

To better understand the needs of potential members and develop their USP, ASQ decided to undertake a project that involved both qualitative and quantitative research. The data generated by this project provided ASQ with a clearer understanding of what potential members wanted: support from the association to help advance their careers in the quality field. It also highlighted that, despite having the products to meet these member needs, ASQ had not adequately made the connection for members on how their portfolio of services could specifically help them achieve

---

[67] Bly, *The Direct Mail Revolution*.

their goal. ASQ had the solutions for members, but members did not understand how to access these opportunities and use them for career development.

As a result of the research, ASQ had a better view of the unique selling proposition to meet the needs of prospective members in their marketplace. Of equal importance, they understood that their marketing and communications had been inadequate to connect these needs with the resources they had available. ASQ started the process of transforming all their communications—from recruitment to renewal to the website—to explain precisely how ASQ can help members "advance [their] career to the next level of excellence."[68] This included building an interactive web tool that allowed prospects, by answering a series of questions, to find which of the 18 certifications ASQ offered would help them in their career.

Qualitative and quantitative research is one very effective method to help you define your association's USP. Another timelier way you can use to refine your USP is the three-step exercise highlighted below. Once completed, a quick test of some of the USPs that you have developed is appropriate. The validation can be done by highlighting a few different value propositions in digital ads and reading the responses. Alternatively, you could divide up your email list and present different value messages to each segment to see which produces the most new members.

Just like ASQ, once you have settled on a USP that best speaks to your target market's needs and aspirations, the next step is determining how to communicate it to prospective members effectively. There are five central building blocks to consider in your membership recruitment communication strategy.

---

[68] "Why ASQ? | ASQ."

TRANSLATING FEATURES AND BENEFITS
INTO A UNIQUE SELLING PROPOSITION

Many membership organizations find developing their USP challenging. Here is a team exercise that helps break down the process into sequential steps to gain a perspective of value from the ground up.

1. To start the exercise, create a list of the features included in your membership. Add as many to the list as come to mind. A feature consists of the specific deliverables in the membership package, like a magazine, career center, and private social network. It sometimes helps to hold and touch these features by placing copies of them on the table for your team to see. For those products that are not tangible, you can print out their descriptions from your website.

2. As a next step, write down the key benefits that each product or service provides to a member. Be specific. For example, the job board of an association's career center is a feature that offers members the benefit of access to a trusted source of jobs, specifically in their field. Similarly, a private online community is a feature that benefits members by helping them to network directly with other professionals in their industry.

3. Now that you have a long list of features and benefits, the next step is translating them into a straightforward value statement. For example, the value statement for the association's magazine ensures you are aware of the hottest topics in your field. The job board will help you get a higher paying position and find the job of your dreams. The value of a private online community is that it allows you to get instant answers to your professional questions from a network of top practitioners.

From these value statements, a common thread will emerge for how membership makes a difference in a member's life, profession, and company. In this example, membership represents an essential guide for growth and advancement in a member's career. This common thread is your value proposition, and because of the step-by-step process you used to get there, you also have the storyline of how your association can deliver on the USP.

CONNECTING WITH EMOTIONAL DRIVERS

After identifying a USP, the next step is communicating it by connecting it with the motivations that drive a member's behavior. Why do members want to advance their careers? Is it to make more money or gain respect and recognition? Understanding these drivers helps you properly frame the value you deliver.

Back in 1956, in his book, *Mail Order Strategy*, Victor Schwab, an *Ad Age* Person of the Century, defined what he saw as 40 key "emotional drivers" that influence people's actions. Here are some of Schwab's drivers that I think might be particularly relevant for membership recruitment.

People want to **be**:
- Up to date
- Recognized authorities
- Efficient
- Good bosses and employers

People want to **gain**:
- Time
- Comfort
- Praise of others
- Health
- Popularity
- Personal prestige
- Money

People want to **save**:
- Work
- Discomfort
- Embarrassment
- Worry
- Time

People want to **do** the following:
- Satisfy their curiosity
- Win others' affection
- Improve themselves generally[69]

---

[69] "22 Emotional Drivers That Influence Consumer Buying Behavior."

Human nature does not change very much, so I believe these drivers are still relevant today. Interestingly, Seth Godin brings a modern-day perspective to Schwab's emotional drivers. He asserts, "You may say you're offering a widget, but don't believe it. When you're marketing change, you're offering a new emotional state, a step closer to the dreams and desires of your customers, not a widget. We sell feelings, status, and connections, not tasks and stuff."[70]

Probably the most successful marketing example of using an emotional driver is *The Wall Street Journal* subscription campaign promising success and status by making a buying decision. The letter, excerpted here, artfully taps into a person's desire to succeed. It says:

> "On a beautiful late spring afternoon, twenty-five years ago, two young men graduated from the same college. They were very much alike, these two young men. Both had been better than average students, both were personable, and both—as young college graduates—were filled with ambitious dreams for the future.
>
> Recently, these men returned to their college for their 25th reunion.
>
> They were very much alike. Both were happily married. Both had three children. And both, it turned out, had gone to work for the same Midwestern manufacturing company, and were still there.
>
> But there was a difference. One of the men was manager of a small department of that company. The other was its president.
>
> What Made the Difference
>
> Have you ever wondered, as I have, what makes this kind of difference in people's lives? It isn't always a native intelligence or talent or dedication. It isn't that one person wants success and the other doesn't.
>
> The difference lies in what each person knows and how he or she makes use of that knowledge.
>
> And that is why I am writing to you and to people like you about *The Wall Street Journal*. For that is the whole purpose of the *Journal*: to give its readers knowledge—knowledge that they can use in business."[71]

---

[70] Godin, *This Is Marketing*.
[71] "The One Letter That Generated $1.5 Billion in Revenues."

CREATING STRONG HEADLINES

Once you have your emotional drivers and have defined specific value, it is time to apply them in your messaging. Your message begins with your headline. Whether it is an email subject line, a Facebook ad, or a landing page on your website, headlines still make a big difference in the effectiveness of your message. Today that may be truer than ever because, with the volume of messages that we receive, more people tend to scan content rather than carefully read every word of your promotion.

David Ogilvy was the founder of the advertising agency Ogilvy & Mather and known as the "Father of Advertising." From a copywriting perspective, he believed the headline was the most influential aspect of any advertising. He was known to have written no fewer than sixteen versions of a headline until he got it right.

His guidance on what makes excellent headlines included the following tips:

- Promise a benefit in your headline like "Save Now."
- Include the keyword identifying your audience or product in your headline: Nurses, Teachers, Engineers, or Membership.
- Inject something newsworthy or a finding into your headlines using words like "Introducing," "Last Chance," and "Announcing."

These classic headline recommendations are timeless. In marketing today, the most likely place for a headline to appear is in the subject line for an email. Here are some modern-day subject lines for membership recruitment that follow Ogilvy's guidance.

- "3 tips for finding a job."
- "An exclusive offer just for you."
- "I found you through your colleague (name)"
- "You're invited to join us!"
- "Have You Heard the News?"
- "Permission to close your file?"

DEVELOPING EFFECTIVE COPY

Your headline is followed by a compelling presentation about the value of membership.

Recruitment marketing's sole goal is to move a prospect
from the position of doing nothing to motivate them to
do something, and that something is deciding to join.

Copy should not be a manual on how membership works or a speech that will last for the ages. Instead, as one of the early direct marketing legends, Claude Hopkins, argued, the greatest weakness in copywriting is that writers "forget they are salesmen and try to be performers. Instead of sales, they seek applause."[72] Recruitment marketing's sole goal is to move a prospect from the position of doing nothing to motivate them to do something, and that something is deciding to join.

Copywriting begins with determining who is the best person to be the "voice" to share your membership message. Should it be the membership director, executive director, or the board president? I recommend that the copy come from the voice of the membership director. Because of their role and interaction with members, a membership person can tell the most compelling and believable stories about how joining can make a difference to someone's career or their company.

As you write copy, keep Hopkins's admonition in mind. Write your marketing copy as a conversation between a salesperson and a prospective member. Ask and answer the questions any prospective member would ask, and be sure to deal directly with typical sales objections like, "It seems to be expensive," or, "Will I find it valuable?" As you write, also be sure to provide specific proof. Support your USP by answering the prospect's question, "How do I know that I can believe you?" with real examples, data, and testimonials.

Copywriter Lois Geller reminds us that "there is one rule of thumb to follow when you're writing ad copy: edit, edit, edit."[73] As you edit, she reminds us to keep sentences short and your writing simple. Use Microsoft Word spelling and grammar to check your document for errors and to see if the readability level is acceptable. Marketing copy typically should not be any higher than the ninth grade reading level. Share your copy with someone who is not familiar with your organization. Can they find your value proposition? Can they see your offer by scanning the text? Is it clear what a prospect needs to do to respond to your invitation? Have you buried your most important message in the body of your promotion? Is the copy convincing and compelling to them?

---

[72] Hopkins, Claude C., *My Life in Advertising and Scientific Advertising* (Advertising Age Classics Library): Claude C. Hopkins: 9780844231013: Amazon.Com: Gateway.
[73] Geller, *Response*.

PRESENTING COMPELLING VISUALS AND GRAPHICS

How you present your message visually has also become more critical today. In digital ads, like those on Facebook, clicks can be substantially increased by trading out a variety of pictures, even while keeping the copy the same. A persuasive testimonial video with captions also generates higher levels of interaction with the ad.

In other recruitment channels, one surprising outcome is that the graphics that often work best are characterized by "less is more." In regular tests of email and direct mail, subdued graphics for an invitation to join seem to work better than bold HTML graphics or four-color printing. For example, a simple "outlook" style email that appears as if it was sent directly by you to a single prospective member from your computer can outperform an email with pictures and bold graphics. In the same way, a personalized letter and reply form in a standard envelope that addresses Mr. Smith directly will do better than a big colorful brochure with pictures of events, products, and other members.

When it comes to membership recruitment, my hypothesis for why simpler graphics seem to do better is that membership is personal and not a mass-market purchase like a car or furniture that requires visuals. Instead, a one-on-one appeal highlighting that an individual is qualified and personally invited to be a member communicates recognition and status. After all, "membership has its privileges."

PROVIDING A CALL TO ACTION

Whether you are creating a promotional email, online ad, direct mail package, or working at an exhibit, the starting point for your effort should be defining what you want the recipient of your message to do. In marketing terms, we call this creating a Call to Action (CTA).

A CTA is a simple statement or visual that informs the person receiving your message exactly what action you want them to take. When someone gets a communication, it is basic human psychology to ask, "What do you want me to do?" A strong CTA answers this question.

At the start of any recruitment promotion, it is vital
to have in mind where you want your prospective member
to go and what you want them to do.

Optimizing your CTA includes reviewing the join page on your website to be sure it is consistent with your message and offer, and that it has clear instructions for users. At the start of any recruitment promotion, it is vital to have in mind where you want your prospective member to go and what you want them to do.

It also means that there are multiple "Join Now" buttons in your email, "Act Now" statements in your direct mail copy, "Can I take your order?" language in your phone scripts, and "Learn More" links in your digital ads. A CTA is essential in every promotion to encourage a prospect to join.

Here are some simple CTA buttons from some popular products:

- Dropbox: Sign Up for Free
- Netflix: Join Free for a Month
- Uber: Sign up to Drive | Start Riding with Uber
- Spotify: Go Premium | Play Free
- Pinterest: Continue with Facebook | Sign Up
- Instagram: Download on the App Store | Get it on Google Play[74]

One association with whom I was working discovered the hard way what can happen without a prominent call to action. When they launched their new website, it omitted the "Join Now" button previously displayed at the top of their home page. Immediately, the number of new members joining dropped off precipitously. The association wondered if something was wrong with the join process on the new site. After checking it out, they found the website working correctly. The membership director suspected the problem was the missing call to action. After a protracted discussion, the web team restored the button to the site, and immediately the membership joins returned to the previous level. The moral of the story: a CTA is essential for membership recruitment success.

THE POWER OF THE RIGHT MESSAGE

Can a marketing message change society's behavior? Claude Hopkins proved that it could. With the increasing use of sugar in American diets, tooth decay had become a real problem. At the time of World War I, dental hygiene was so bad that the army declared it a national security risk.[75]

At that time, Claude Hopkins agreed to create a marketing campaign for Pepsodent Toothpaste. Toothpaste was available to the public from many suppliers but rarely used. To figure out a compelling message, Hopkins dove into dental research, and he found the value proposition and emotional driver that he was looking to use. "In the middle of one book I

---

[74] Leaning, "31 Call-to-Action Examples You Can't Help But Click."
[75] "The Minty Fresh Psychology Behind America's Toothpaste Obsession."

found a reference to the mucin plaques on teeth, which I afterward called the film. . . . I resolved to advertise this tooth paste as a creator of beauty. To deal with that cloudy film."[76] With that premise, Hopkins began testing ad copy by producing hundreds of ads with coded coupons to determine the exact images and text that worked best. Previously toothpaste had been marketed by scaring people about tooth decay. Hopkins resolved to take the opposite approach. He said, "I learned that beauty was the chief appeal. Most men and women desired to be attractive. When I could offer a convincing way, they listened to my arguments. So I came to feature beauty."[77]

On top of that, to enhance sales further, he tested what he called "altruistic advertising." He began to produce ads that made free samples of Pepsodent Toothpaste available to the public to help build the habit of brushing. The result of these campaigns was that, in a matter of years, Hopkins claimed that Pepsodent had gone from a brand-new product to producing millions of dollars in profits. What's more, later analysis has shown that "Pepsodent became one of the most sold products in the world. The number of regular toothbrushers jumped from 7 percent to 65 percent a decade after the first ad."[78] His marketing messages helped change society's behaviors and made a significant impact on public health.

Developing your association's message may not be world-changing, but the right appeal can have a powerful impact on your membership recruitment. The *Membership Marketing Benchmarking Report* highlights that, on average, both individual and trade associations maintain stable renewal rates of over 80 percent. Once members discover and use the benefits that an association provides, the vast majority will continue their membership for years. Associations have the "steak," but may not effectively communicate the "sizzle" of the outstanding content, products, and services that they provide. By understanding the needs of potential members and sharing the unique value that they deliver to meet those needs (i.e., the compelling message), associations can effectively encourage and provide the push needed to move prospects to become members.

In the next chapter, we will bring together targeting the right prospects with the best offer and using the proper channels and messages to optimize your membership recruitment efforts.

---

[76] Hopkins, Claude C., *My Life in Advertising and Scientific Advertising* (Advertising Age Classics Library): Claude C. Hopkins: 9780844231013: Amazon.Com: Gateway.

[77] Hopkins, Claude C.

[78] "The Minty Fresh Psychology Behind America's Toothpaste Obsession."

CHAPTER NINE

TESTING, TRACKING, AND ANALYSIS – HOW DO YOU OPTIMIZE RECRUITMENT?

Claude Hopkins is acknowledged as the great-grandfather of direct marketing and, as discussed in the previous chapter, successfully used advertising messages to impact society. However, he may best be known for his 1923 book, *Scientific Advertising*. Hopkins maintained that in the past, "advertising was then a gamble—a speculation of the rashest sort. One man's guess on the proper course was as likely to be as good as another's." In contrast, he asserted that "the time has come when advertising has in some hands reached the status of a science." Hopkins then went on to describe how testing and tracking should be the foundation for all marketing efforts. The philosophy that he advanced was: "We learn the principles and prove them by repeated tests. . . We compare one way with many others, backward and forward, and record the results. When one method invariably proves best, that method becomes a fixed principle."[79]

Testing and analysis move marketing from opinions and hunches to a platform of efficiency and professionalism. Marketing becomes an exciting scientific laboratory where ideas and theories can be proposed and validated.

Hopkins effectively outlined the critical steps for conducting regular tests, tracking the results, and applying what works best. Today these

---

[79] Hopkins, Claude C., *My Life in Advertising and Scientific Advertising* (Advertising Age Classics Library): Claude C. Hopkins: 9780844231013: Amazon.Com: Gateway.

principles may be even more urgent than ever because of the number of lists, offers, and channels available to associations. With so many marketing options, testing can mean the difference between discovering significant opportunities to grow your membership or ongoing struggles with a poorly performing program. It can change the culture of an organization. Testing and analysis move marketing from opinions and hunches to a platform of efficiency and professionalism. Marketing becomes an exciting scientific laboratory where ideas and theories can be proposed and validated.

Despite the importance of harnessing testing to build an effective recruitment program, the reality is that many associations struggle with putting the practice into place. According to survey results, only one-third of associations do any head-to-head market testing comparing one approach to another. Similarly, associations are failing to capture source codes for results analysis. Furthermore, only 11 percent of associations do a post-campaign matchback of results to see what efforts were most productive.[80]

The lack of testing, tracking, and analysis means that it is probable that a membership recruitment program is sub-optimizing the potential returns by 100 percent or more.

For one well-known association without testing and tracking in place, a consultant discovered during a year-end analysis that fully a third of the lists that they had used had a zero percent response rate. Yet those lists had repeatedly been mailed, effectively flushing thousands of marketing dollars down the drain. In this case, tracking the results would have allowed the association to reprogram those funds for productive efforts.

MARKETING TESTING

If testing is so important, then how should it be done? There are two steps in the process of establishing effective marketing tests. The first is deciding what to test. Next is properly structuring tests that provide valid results.

The "art" of testing starts with brainstorming and thinking about creative ways to present your membership. In his landmark book, *Successful Direct Marketing Methods*, Bob Stone recommends a series of questions that I have modified for membership recruitment. You can use the questions to help get your creativity started.

- What is new and exciting about the membership?

---

[80] Rossell, Wasserman, and Kerr, "The Membership Marketing Benchmarking Report, 12th Edition."

- Can early bird responders get a special deal?
- Should one of the member benefits be highlighted above all others?
- What visuals will help to present the membership?
- Who should the message come from (staff, board, spokesperson)?
- Does seasonal timing have an impact?
- Is there a way to make joining more straightforward or painless?
- What marketing channels should be tried?
- How does our membership compare to other associations (strengths and weaknesses)?
- Does membership make something easier in someone's life or career?
- Can the message be tied with upcoming events?
- What might be the most confusing aspect of membership in the mind of a prospect?
- What analogies or stories can strengthen the message?[81]

In your brainstorming, do not be afraid to explore and adapt ideas from the marketing efforts that you see all around you. What can you learn from case studies of other associations' recruitment efforts? How are publishers marketing subscriptions? What do companies with renewable products (e.g., Netflix, Amazon Prime, American Express) do to get new members? When do retailers market most aggressively?

Finally, there are some specific high leverage areas to consider testing. These opportunity areas include:

Marketing Lists

One of the elementary and most productive tests is trying new lists. As described in chapter five, a marketing list is a group of individuals definable by behavior, demographics, job titles, industry, or source. It is not uncommon for one list to produce responses five times better than another list. For example, your lapsed membership list will likely outperform a file of registered users from your website, but it may not do as well as recent website cart abandons. Testing lists gives you the answer to who are the best candidates to recruit. Testing also allows you to monitor how broadly you can reach out with your promotions beyond your core market and still get an acceptable return on investment. You may not be achieving your full potential because, without testing new lists and monitoring results, you may be missing new market segments that would respond positively to your membership offer. The best place to get started with testing is by trying new lists.

---

[81] Stone, *Successful Direct Marketing Methods.*

Special Offers

What incentive you make available to encourage a prospect to join can double or triple the responses of your promotion. Chapter six outlined a series of offers that have traditionally produced reliable new member results. Testing can allow you to find out what specific offer works best for your association. By including a test option with no special offer at all, you can also demonstrate the positive economic impact of adding incentives and deals in your recruitment efforts.

Pricing and Discounts

Psychological price points are for real. As a rule of thumb, a price ending in a "7" or a "9" will generate more responses and more revenue than a price ending in a zero. To a large extent, association dues levels are locked in each year, but if you are testing a discount offer or considering raising dues, take advantage of psychological price points by, for example, setting the price at $197 instead of $200.

Packaging

Look for ways to test a bundling or unbundling of your membership offering to see what works best for your association. Several years ago, the Water Environment Federation (WEF) evaluated how best to package their membership. Traditionally, they offered a basic membership with the option of adding on several additional publications. As a test, WEF promoted the traditional membership offer against a bundle that included all the optional periodicals automatically included in the membership dues. The result was that the response rate remained constant, but the average dues paid by a member increased substantially.

Channel and Media Mix

With the variety of marketing channels available today, take advantage of the opportunity to test what combination works best. Try direct mail followed by an email linked to a microsite; then, compare this to a standalone email or mailing. In a test conducted by one association, they divided the prospect audience into two segments. One only received a direct mail membership solicitation. The second group received the same piece plus a follow-up email. The mail-only group responded at a 1.23 percent rate. The combined mail and email group produced a 2.08 percent response rate. For this organization, by combining marketing channels, the test yielded a 69 percent lift in the overall response.

Messaging

Testing different copy and presentations of your value can influence response rates by 50 percent or more. Try new messages that focus on a different emotional driver like saving time or money, or personal growth through membership. An easy and fast way to test approach can be with email subject lines. Send out emails to a small portion of the list with a variety of subject lines. The group with the highest open rate wins, and that subject line goes to the remainder of the list.

Graphics and Formats

We live in a visually driven culture. Often a picture is indeed worth a thousand words. So, how you visually present your membership message in digital ads, email, and direct mail powerfully influences responses. Pictures or videos used in digital ads on social media platforms show the most dramatic changes in response. Email tests offer almost instant feedback based on clicks, opens, and sales. Email graphics can be subtle with text only or bold with pictures, videos, and animations. Direct mail presents even more options in terms of sizes and shapes—from postcards to three-dimensional packages to standard business letters. Based on the test results that I have seen, the best package format to begin testing with is a standard business envelope package.

Once you have developed a good set of test options, it is time to prioritize them. The key here is to test big things first. Look for a breakthrough win in testing that will make a significant difference in your marketing. Testing small changes like colors, fonts, and minor copy updates will have such a minimal impact on the results that the chances are likely that it will not produce a statistically valid outcome. Planning for a test also requires that you do an economic and fulfillment reality check to see if your creative idea is viable. If you usually get a 1 percent response rate, but you plan to try a costly marketing test effort that would require you to achieve a 20 percent response rate for your test to produce the ROI you need, then reconsider. It is unlikely that any test will raise results by a factor of twenty. Similarly, make sure that you can operationally deliver on whatever offers you choose to test without significant disruption to your staff or IT department.

Equally necessary to the art of testing is the "science" of testing. The science of testing starts with creating proper test structures. Valid testing requires drawing a portion of names out of your prospect lists and sending your test effort to them while delivering the bulk of your prospects the existing "control" promotion. Ideally, the test and control efforts are identical except for the variable that you intend to test. For example, if you want to see if a discount offer will improve results, then send out the control (without the discount) and the test (featuring the discount). At the same time, hold the other elements constant by using the same channel and basic value proposition for both the control portion of the list and the test segment.

A test does not always produce better returns than the existing control, so tests should only go to small segments of a broader promotion to minimize risk.

Additionally, you will want to structure the test so that it is statistically valid, which means you can expect the results to be repeatable in future marketing efforts. Statistical validity is determined not by the number of people sent the test but by the number of responses. Marketers argue over the number of responses required for statistical validity. The level you choose will largely depend on the returns you typically get and on how risk-averse your organization is. Many marketers, including the automated marketing platform HubSpot, recommend testing with an 85 percent confidence level. An 85 percent confidence level and a 25 percent margin of error will require that you have enough names in each test segment to achieve 14 responses. A 90 percent confidence level will require 26 replies, and a 95 percent confidence level will require 42 responses, all with a 25 percent margin of error.

Here is a sample test structure for a multi-segment marketing test.

SAMPLE TEST GRID

LIST NAME	TOTAL COUNT	CONTROL	TEST 1	TEST 2
LAPSED	15,000	7,500	3,750	3,750
CUSTOMERS	12,000	6,000	3,000	3,000
RENTED	10,000	5,000	2,500	2,500
TOTAL	37,000	18,500	9,250	9,250

MARKETING TRACKING

The other required component in the science of testing is tracking. For many associations tracking their marketing results is a serious challenge. Associations report that the top data challenge they face is their lack of marketing results tracking and analysis.[82] Marketing without tracking results is like a pilot flying an aircraft without knowing the altitude, speed, heading, and wind direction. It is a formula for disaster. What is more, the potential upside for an organization to build sustainable growth through marketing tracking is so enormous that one way or another, it needs to support the development of this infrastructure.

Many groups have been able to establish tracking systems successfully. The most effective tracking mechanisms that associations use to capture and evaluate marketing results include:

Source Code Tracking

Using a source code or offer code is the most basic form of tracking responses. This unique identifier is included in every recruitment effort and is required to be entered by the prospect to receive whatever special offer you make available. If the respondent mails in a membership application, the code should be entered into the member's record. If the prospect joins online prompted by an email, entering it is required to receive the offer. Print and digital ads can also use source codes. The weakness in this tracking method is that some respondents will not use the information when they join. However, with a valuable offer as the incentive, enough data can still be collected to make sound marketing decisions.

Matchback Tracking

A more sophisticated tracking method is performing a matchback of new members against the original promotion lists used in a recruitment campaign. With this method, you still assign source codes to identify files and offers, but when a new member joins, you also match them back to the original prospect list. The source code of those who match is assigned to the new member's record. No action is required by the member when joining. For lower volume marketing efforts, you can do this matchback process with a spreadsheet comparing the new members against the prospect list. With higher volumes of prospects and new members, you

---

[82] In response to the *Membership Marketing Benchmarking Report* question "What are the most significant data challenges your association faces?" the top response at 39 percent of respondents was the "lack of marketing results tracking and analysis reporting."

will want to use merge-purge software that matches names, addresses, and emails between your prospect list and new member list.

Google Tag Manager Tracking

With more and more sales coming to websites through digital marketing, Google Tag Manager is becoming a significant tracking opportunity. It allows you to place tracking URLs and tags on your email campaigns and digital ads to monitor the path a prospect takes to complete a purchase. Once a prospect joins, the trigger for the tag fires, alerting you to the response.

Whether you use spreadsheets, sophisticated software, or Google Tag Manager, the tools to track recruitment results are advancing. By using these tools, the opportunity is to move recruitment beyond the lament attributed to the retail merchant John Wanamaker who famously said: "Half the money I spend on advertising is wasted; the trouble is I don't know which half." Instead, well-designed tracking methods allow you to target and optimize your recruitment efforts for maximum effectiveness.

MARKETING ANALYSIS

Once testing and tracking are in place, the world of analysis opens to associations. An association can determine what lists and market segments are the best targets, what offers drive response, what channels are most effective, and how to best present the value provided by the association. This knowledge is power.

Let's look at some of the specific analysis options that are useful for evaluating recruitment efforts.

RESPONSE RATE

measures the number of prospects who responded to a marketing effort.

| TOTAL NUMBER OF RESPONSES | TOTAL NUMBER OF PROSPECTS CONTACTED | MULTIPLIED BY 100 |

The most basic analytical tool is calculating the response rate for a promotion. The formula for calculating a response rate is to divide the number of responses by the number of prospects receiving the promotion and then multiply that number by 100 to produce a percentage. If a campaign generated 155 new members and went to 10,000 potential members, then the response rate would be 1.55 percent. If the marketing effort included a test, calculating the response rate will identify what worked best. For example, if the test segment went to 2,500 and produced 50 returns, the response rate would be 2.00 percent. And if the control segment went to 7,500 and generated 105 new members, the response rates would be 1.40 percent. The same method can also be used for each list used in the promotion to compare results and see which worked best.

Measuring results by response rate works well if the dues amount and the promotional costs are the same for each list or test in the promotion. For example, if an email goes out with a message test to a house list and the dues rate is the same, then the segment with the highest response rate wins. However, if the test is an expensive direct mail package run against an inexpensive postcard, even if the test has a higher response rate, it may not be the winner because of the difference in printing, mailing, and postage costs.

COST PER ACQUISITION (CPA)

measures the average cost to obtain a new member.

ACQUISITION
COSTS

MEMBERS
ACQUIRED

That is why doing an analysis based solely on the response rate may be insufficient to get an accurate read on the results. Instead, with variable promotion costs, calculating the Cost Per Acquisition (CPA) is an even more precise measure of effectiveness. The CPA takes the expense of the promotion and divides it by the number of new members obtained. Using the examples above, if the postcard went to 7,500 prospects and the cost was $3,000, the CPA for that segment would be $28.57 ($3,000/105). For the direct mail test package going to 2,500, with a cost of $2,000, the CPA would be $40 ($2,000/50). One variable to add to this evaluation would be to extrapolate what the cost and number of responses would have been if the more expensive direct mail package had gone to the same quantity as the postcard (7,500). This extra step would equalize the cost since, in direct mail, increased volumes lower the per piece price.

The most sophisticated recruitment analysis method is measuring results based on Return on Investment (ROI). Doing an ROI analysis considers both the cost and the revenue produced by a promotion. This approach can look at both the short-term results for each recruitment campaign, but more importantly, it can highlight the long-term impact. As previously discussed, membership recruitment has a different economic model than most products offered by an association. Membership produces a recurring revenue stream.

In the short term, ROI is necessary to consider if an association has variable dues amounts. The International Public Management Association for Human Resources (IPMA-HR), for example, makes two membership categories available. Potential members can join as an individual or sign up their entire HR department. Dues vary from $149 for an individual member to up to $3,870 for the full department. Because of this price variance, IPMA-HR is willing to accept a much higher CPA to obtain an organizational member. For an accurate analysis, they measure recruitment returns based on ROI. They calculate the CPA for a promotion, and they capture the total revenue for both the control effort and the test. The CPA is then subtracted from the revenue to provide the ROI obtained for each member.

Following our example above, if the individual and organizational memberships are both offered in the promotion, and the postcard's average dues are $200 with the CPA of $28.57, then the ROI per new member would be $171.43. If the average dues from new members for the direct mail piece are $500 and the CPA is $40 then the ROI per member is $460. Using the ROI analysis incorporating both the variable costs and revenue highlights that the winner in this example is the direct mail package over the postcard.

For long-term recruitment analysis, knowing the ROI generated from membership recruitment efforts provides the basis for calculating the lifetime value of a member and the maximum acquisition cost discussed in chapter four.

Building reports to track response rates, CPA, and ROI takes time and effort. However, once understood, you can build the formulas into spreadsheets or other software to automate the process. This analysis will lay the foundation for an efficient and effective recruitment effort that documents the economic vitality of your membership marketing.

NEXT STEPS

One of the famous quotes from business writer Tom Peters is, "life is pretty simple: you do some stuff. Most fails. Some works. If it works big, then you do something else. The trick is the doing something else." The thought is appropriate when considering optimizing your membership recruitment efforts. Without employing the marketing methods discussed in this chapter, inefficiencies and underperformance are guaranteed for your program. However, by establishing an organizational priority on testing, tracking, and analysis, you will understand what works and what fails, and you will have the opportunity to grow your membership and advance the mission of your association.

PART THREE

SUSTAINING **GROWTH** AND **RESILIENCY**

CHAPTER TEN

THE NEED
FOR INNOVATION

When I do presentations on the need for innovation, I often share a comparison of Sears and Amazon as a case study. There may not be a better example of the implications of whether or not organizations innovate and embrace change.

In July of 1995, when Amazon first opened its online store, Sears possessed everything needed to become what Amazon is today and more. Sears had a dominant and trusted brand. They sold a full portfolio of products, from clothes to appliances to tools. Sears had an enormous print catalog along with an extensive customer list and warehouses to pack and ship purchases. In fact, for over one hundred years, Sears mailed out its big book catalog to a significant portion of the U.S. population. At times, the catalog was as large as 1,500 pages and offered more than 100,000 products.

Even a decade after Amazon came on the scene, Sears still held many advantages. In 2007, Sears had sales of $53 billion and had 350,000 employees, while Amazon had sales of $14 billion and 17,000 employees. However, those advantages were not to last long. By 2018, Sears filed for bankruptcy as sales dropped to $16 billion, and staffing fell to 89,000. By that time, Amazon sales had soared to $232 billion, with over 600,000 employees.

So, what happened? Those who have done in-depth studies of the demise of Sears point to several factors, including the emergence of discount retailers like Walmart and category-focused retailers like Home Depot and Best Buy. But a massive contributor to Sears's challenge was their failure to capitalize on the movement to online shopping, leaving the door open for Amazon to capture this market. Their lack of innovation and adaptation in pricing and product focus, combined with its delay in moving from brick and mortar to the internet, spelled disaster for this retail giant.

> If you do everything recommended in this book to drive growth through effective recruitment but do not use that growth to support innovation, your organization will ultimately reach a point of steady state and even decline.

There are lessons from the Sears experience that can be applied to not only for-profit companies but to membership organizations. Here is the lesson. If you do everything recommended in this book to drive growth through effective recruitment but do not use that growth to support innovation, your organization will ultimately reach a point of steady state and even decline.

In practical terms, this flattening of the membership growth curve happens because, by effectively marketing to prospects in your chosen field, you will ultimately reach a point of market saturation. In effect, you become a victim of your own success. You have reached the prospective members who were interested in joining and even succeeded in getting those who were on the fence to become members. You have fully penetrated your prospect market. What's more, without investing in new product development, even the loyal members you have added will become bored and lose their excitement for the benefits that you provide.

In short, without a focus on innovation, just like Sears or any maturing organization, growth will be stunted, and membership will begin to diminish.

SUSTAINING THE MEMBERSHIP GROWTH CURVE

So how can a membership organization sustain vitality and growth? One of the most-read articles on organizational resiliency by Gary Hamel and Liisa Välikangas in the *Harvard Business Review* put it simply, "Strategic resilience is not about responding to a one-time crisis. It's not about rebounding from a setback. It's about continuously anticipating and adjusting to deep, secular trends that can permanently impair the earning power of a core business. It's about having the capacity to change before the case for change becomes desperately obvious."[83] As these authors concluded, "A turnaround is transformation tragically delayed."

---

[83] "The Quest for Resilience."

> Associations with membership increases in the past year, and over the last five years, are significantly more likely to report that their organization has a culture that supports innovation.

Research conducted with nearly a thousand associations supports this conclusion. Associations with membership increases in the past year, and over the last five years, are significantly more likely to report that their organization has a culture that supports innovation. Conversely, those reporting declines in membership are considerably more likely to share that their organization is only slightly innovative or not innovative at all.[84]

There is no single recipe for successful innovation. As Matt Ridley noted in his book, *How Innovation Works,* "Innovation is not an individual phenomenon, but a collective, incremental and messy network phenomenon."[85] However, there are some methods that associations have used successfully to drive new ideas and maintain relevance in an ever-changing environment. These innovative methods include keeping a focus on seeing big-picture opportunities, using marketing research to monitor member needs and perceptions, seeking outside perspectives, and—very simply—trying lots of new ideas.

KEEPING THE BIG PICTURE IN VIEW

Maintaining a big-picture perspective is one of the most significant steps for identifying new ideas and opportunities. However, everything in our daily life seems to pull us toward the details and incremental solutions. The proverb "You can't see the forest for the trees" captures this challenge. We tend to develop ever more granular solutions to try and fix a problem without stepping back and looking at the big picture and a high leverage solution.

Overcoming this myopic tendency is often a struggle for associations. For example, one of the often-repeated tenets in association marketing is that segmentation of members and prospects into ever smaller groups will produce better results. The theory says that highly targeted messages sent to each segment detailing specifics about the association's benefits and services will solve a membership decline. You might hear something like, "If we tell the prospects that we publish articles in their specialty, then they will join." One association with whom we have worked, which has no more than 7,000 members, is continually under pressure from its board

---

[84] Rossell, Wasserman, and Kerr, "The Membership Marketing Benchmarking Report, 12th Edition."
[85] RIdley, *How Innovation Works*.

to do just this kind of segmentation. They want to present differentiated services to a dozen subgroups. Besides the complexity in managing this type of program, the real issue is that by trying to serve these limited segments, an association can take its eye off the big picture and the more significant marketplace trends. Through their push for ever-finer divisions, they may accomplish the very opposite results of what they were hoping to achieve. Even if the message encourages a prospect to join by highlighting specific information as soon as they receive a copy of their first magazine and newsletter, they will see that the membership they purchased is not what they expected.

That is why one innovation method to achieve continued growth is to go in the exact opposite direction and focus on the forest and not the trees. Instead of focusing efforts on more granular segmentation, seek out the value needed by your broader audience. As one author advised, "think noncustomers before customers; commonalities before differences; and desegmentation before pursuing finer segmentation."[86] By identifying the broader needs in the marketplace, you have the opportunity to realize extraordinary possibilities.

The American Association for the Advancement of Science (AAAS) made this strategic decision to go big. AAAS is a multidisciplinary organization serving scientists, engineers, and educators with their flagship magazine, *Science.* One membership growth option would have been to segment the market by the scientific specialty of members. In doing so, they would have entered into competition with hundreds of specialty associations. Instead, AAAS decided to reach the broader market of perhaps millions of people who were interested in science but did not have the background to benefit from their existing, more in-depth publication. Hence, AAAS created a science advocacy membership and provided these members a newsletter, *Science on Tap*, that curated the week's scientific news in an easy-to-digest format.

Similarly, Amazon launched its business as an online discount book retailer. They could have stopped there and simply provided specialized services to book buyers. Instead, they used their highly efficient infrastructure to broaden their product offerings. The result was outstanding growth. In the next chapter, I will look at how some associations have achieved exponential growth by looking at larger opportunities and expanding to new markets.

---

[86] Kim and Mauborgne, *Blue Ocean Strategy.*

USING MARKET RESEARCH

Keeping your membership offerings thriving also requires staying on top of the trends and demands of the markets you serve. Market research is a tool to keep your finger on the pulse of these opportunities. Regularly conducted qualitative research, whether in-person or online focus groups or in-depth interviews, provides meaningful directional information. Additionally, quantitative research offers statistical validation when evaluating new opportunities. Consistently deployed, these tools provide data on long-term trends that you may miss with a one-off research snapshot.

Market research helps an association monitor the evolution and even the revolution that is taking place in its field or industry by seeking answers to questions like:

- What are the emerging trends, discoveries, and technologies in the field?
- How are members' titles and job functions changing?
- How useful are the current member benefits, and how well is the association delivering on them?
- What are the strengths and weaknesses of proposed new products and services?
- What are the shortcomings of the existing membership model?
- What are the optimal prices for new membership categories and products?
- How does the membership compare to what is offered by other associations or companies?

By understanding and capturing what is going on in an industry, an association can stay ahead of the competition and aggressively take hold of new market opportunities.

SEEKING AN OUTSIDE PERSPECTIVE

Dr. William Osler, one of the founders of Johns Hopkins Hospital, famously said, "A physician who treats himself has a fool for a patient." The quote should be an excellent reminder to us as membership marketers. We, as individuals, and our organizations, have blind spots and do not always have a clear vision of the opportunities and challenges in front of us.

So, another innovation opportunity is to aggressively seek insight and guidance from others to maintain a resilient program. This need becomes more important each passing day as the level of expertise needed to manage membership marketing is at an all-time high with the increasing availability of marketing channels, more sophisticated data analysis tools, and new regulations and laws. Getting guidance can come in a variety of forms, including attending and networking at professional development events, bringing consultants or contractors on board, or hiring a marketing agency. Each of these options provides valuable insights.

There are numerous in-person and online learning opportunities for membership professionals. The one-on-one interactions at these events, combined with the presentations, are a great way to learn from the successes and failures of other associations. Over time you can build a network of colleagues who can bring perspectives to help you with complex, controversial, or politically sensitive questions.

A consultant or contractor can also supplement your existing team. There are times when the tasks are too complex, or the workload is too much for your staff. It might be because of special projects, vacancies, or unexpected events. Theoretically, an association could carry staff for all these situations, but this adds year-round costs for salary, benefits, software, and office space. A consultant can join your team to help your staff through this time and then move on to the next assignment when the project is over.

You can also drive innovation by working with a marketing agency. If you need a medical procedure, you would be wise to look for the doctor that has done the surgery successfully many times. You want the doctor with the best specialized skills and knowledge. In the same way, an experienced marketing agency is composed of a team with proven skills ranging from strategy development, to project management, to results analysis. When there is an important assignment or program that requires particular knowledge or expertise, a marketing agency that has effectively accomplished the assignment dozens of times with other organizations might be just what the doctor ordered.

TRYING LOTS OF IDEAS

A final key to maintaining resilience for a membership organization is continuing to focus on innovation by always trying a lot of new ideas. Hamel and Välikangas concluded their *Harvard Business Review* article with this advice. "Most companies would be better off if they made fewer billion-dollar bets and a whole lot more $10,000 or $20,000 bets—some of which will, in time, justify more substantial commitments. They should steer clear of grand, imperial strategies and devote themselves instead to launching a swarm of low-risk experiments."[87] Not every new idea will be a winner, but building this innovation practice into an association's culture will ultimately lead to success. As the great inventor and innovator Thomas Edison famously said, "invention is 1 percent inspiration and 99 percent perspiration." His methodology was always trial and error. For example, "In developing the nickel-iron battery, his employees undertook 50,000 experiments."[88]

In the association world, a remarkable example of this is the American Association of Airport Executives (AAAE). In 1983, AAAE would have been considered a fairly small association by almost any standard. AAAE had an annual budget of $600,000 and a staff of five. The leadership understood the importance of growth to serve the membership and accomplish the association's mission in the aviation industry. However, AAAE determined that growth would not come from raising member dues. Instead, they committed to seeking revenue through innovation and entrepreneurship.

The commitment to innovation probably succeeded beyond even the association's leadership expectations. Through their initiatives, AAAE created a portfolio of products and services that dramatically addressed the airport industry's needs and produced substantial revenue to support the association's mission. As a result, AAAE has expanded its staff to over 80, and the most recently reported budget for the association and foundation is over $100 million. What's more, member dues only make up about 3 percent of this budget. The revenue growth has come from the development of a portfolio of new products and services to support AAAE's members. In addition to the typical association benefits, the association has created many out-of-the-box solutions to serve members' broad industry needs, including:

- The Digicast training system that gives thousands of airport employees on-demand video training on every aspect needed to run

---

[87] "The Quest for Resilience."
[88] Ridley, *How Innovation Works.*

an airport, including operations, maintenance, security, customer service, and human resources.

- The Airport Innovation Index that allows airports to quickly find and learn about significant projects which are currently in progress or completed at other airports.
- The PASS+ digital signage system that helps speed airline passengers through screening checkpoints by giving them timely information tailored specifically to a member airport.

In 2019, AAAE announced that it had reached a record high membership for the association's 91-year history. This growth represents a 24 percent increase over the past five years. Because of the development of valuable products and services, AAAE was able to meet the goal of keeping membership dues well below the industry average for professional associations to make it affordable for everyone in the aviation industry to join at any stage of their career.[89]

MISSING THE OPPORTUNITY TO CHANGE

Unfortunately, just like there are real-world outcomes for organizations that innovate and adapt, there are also stories of those that have not. The paths of two associations, described in broad terms below, serve as an example of the opportunities and challenges faced when the environment changes around an industry.

At the start of the 21st century, some of the leadership of the Special Libraries Association (SLA) came to realize that their name was too narrow in defining the roles and responsibilities of current and prospective members. With technological changes, many members no longer had "librarian" in their job titles and did not work in traditional libraries. The association needed to offer a "bigger tent" solution and appeal to non-librarians. To address the misperceptions posed by the existing name, SLA held votes in 2003, and again in 2009, proposing a name change to reflect the new reality. In each instance, the vote failed, representing—at least in part—a failure of the organization to adapt and speak to a wider audience and serve a more diverse membership. From 2008 to 2011, the association fell on hard times, experiencing a drop in its revenue of 30 percent. As membership declined and the association continued to have financial difficulties, they reduced staff from 28 to 12.[90] Finally, SLA transitioned from a stand-alone association and moved to an association management firm. Since then, SLA has continued to serve this select group of librarians

---

[89] "History."
[90] "Association Finances."

faithfully, so one could argue that they have been faithful to their original mission. However, the path of not changing was painful and the possibility of providing services to a broader audience, who provide information and research services to companies around the globe, may have been missed.

In contrast, the National Burglar & Fire Alarm Association (NBFAA) saw the transformation taking place in their industry and embraced innovation. In 2009, witnessing the changes in electronic security technology and consumer needs, NBFAA members voted to change the association's name to the Electronic Security Association (ESA). The name change significantly expanded the market appeal of the association beyond manufacturers of fire alarms to include technology companies focused on connecting homes and businesses to the internet like Honeywell, Ring, and Verizon. ESA member companies now employ more than 500,000 and serve more than 34 million residential and commercial clients.

In the next chapter, we will explore two successful methods that associations have employed to maintain resilience and growth through the strategies of market expansion and new product development.

CHAPTER ELEVEN

MEMBERSHIP INNOVATION OPPORTUNITIES

Two primary innovation strategies have powered resiliency for associations. The first involves moving into adjacent new markets that might be appropriate for your membership offering. This strategy is known as a market expansion strategy. Successfully reaching and serving new markets can lead to substantial growth.

The second innovation is a product line extension strategy. This method involves adapting your membership model to better fit the wants and needs of prospects in your current marketplace.

A simple quadrant matrix highlights these opportunities, with the top left quadrant representing your current market and membership product. The market expansion quadrant is taking your existing membership into a new market. The bottom left quadrant represents updating your membership product in your current market. Typically, the fourth quadrant at the bottom right, highlights offering a brand-new membership product to a new market. This strategy would represent a significant risk that few associations have successfully implemented.

QUADRANT GROWTH CHART

MARKETS

PRODUCTS		CURRENT	NEW
	CURRENT	Status Quo	Market Expansion
	NEW	Product Expansion	Diversification

MARKET EXPANSION STRATEGY

Perhaps the best example of a successful market expansion strategy by an association is one deployed by AARP. The organization was formed in 1947 by Dr. Ethel Percy Andrus, a retired high school principal. Initially, its mission was to serve retired educators under the name of the National Retired Teachers Association (NRTA). Because the introduction of Medicare was still nearly 20 years away, insurance was often hard to obtain for older adults. To meet this need, one of the primary benefits NRTA provided was a member insurance program.

However, after ten years of operation, in 1958, NRTA rebranded itself as the American Association of Retired Persons (AARP) when Andrus opened the organization to all senior Americans. This expansion beyond retired educators sparked extraordinary membership growth from 50,000 members in 1958 to 1.6 million members by 1978. Then, in 1984, AARP membership further expanded its reach by lowering the age of eligibility from 55 to 50. This change again resulted in growth, and by 1988, AARP membership reached 30 million.[91] Today, individuals can join AARP at any age, and membership numbers have grown to over 38 million.

AARP's growth was supported by favorable demographics, the market's need for insurance, and a good membership value proposition. Nevertheless, if AARP did not expand its view of the markets it served by going beyond its original narrow teacher market, and by broadening the

---

[91] "The Empire Called AARP Under Its Nonprofit Halo, the American Association of Retired Persons Is a Feared Lobbyist and an Even More Awesome Marketer. - October 1, 1988."

age range of membership, some other organization would be serving seniors today instead. The association's market expansion strategy was the foundation for its growth.

Just like AARP's success in moving beyond the teacher market to embrace all older adults, other associations have also found success in redefining the potential members that they can serve. Expanding to new markets was a key driver of membership growth for the Association for Supervision and Curriculum Development (ASCD). In the early 1980s, ASCD was a 12,000-member organization publishing educational research to support curriculum development staff in school district offices. Their market consisted of perhaps 40,000 prospects. However, through membership recruitment testing, ASCD found that school principals also had a desire to access this research to stay on top of the new ideas in teaching and learning. They responded favorably to ASCD's membership invitations. This outreach opened a new market of over 100,000 prospects and drove membership up over 300 percent.

Efforts to reach new markets did not stop with effectively offering school principals membership. Next, ASCD began to reach out to the department heads and teachers in schools. Through these outreaches to the classroom teacher market segment, ASCD grew its membership to 135,000, a ten-fold increase from where they had been by only serving their core market.[92]

To serve these diverse groups, ASCD adjusted its benefits package over time to make membership more accessible to these new markets. More significantly, what they did was to help the members connect the dots between the latest research in learning and how it applied in the classroom. This combination of theory and practice provided value to the broad educational marketplace.

Benchmarking data highlights the impact of successfully reaching out to younger members. Associations with increases in their one-year and five-year membership numbers are more likely to have higher percentages of Millennials and Generation X members.

Similarly, like AARP who realized growth by reaching out to younger members, many associations are thriving through innovative ways to attract and provide value to Millennials and Generation X members.

Benchmarking data highlights the impact of successfully reaching out to younger members. Associations with increases in their one-year and five-year membership numbers are more likely to have higher percentages

---

[92] "ASCD Annual Report."

of Millennials and Generation X members. One way these groups are achieving this is by offering a young professional program and more vehicles for members to interact with the association on digital platforms like online learning. Conversely, associations reporting no growth or declines in their membership in the past year are significantly more likely to have a higher proportion of Baby Boomers as members.[93]

Young members should be an attractive market for associations. In research conducted for Personify titled, "Young Members 2.0," a thousand Millennials and Generation X members highlighted their affinity for association membership. "Across the board young members remain steadfast in their commitment to membership with 87 percent of those responding [saying] it is important to be part of an association and more than half (51%) reported being part of an association is becoming more important than it used to be."

PRODUCT LINE EXPANSION STRATEGY

The second innovation strategy that has resulted in significant membership growth for associations is changing their membership model. A term to describe this strategy is product line extension. *The Oxford Press Marketing Dictionary* defines this as "adding depth to an existing product line by introducing new products in the same product category; product line extensions give customers greater choice and help to protect the firm from a flanking attack by a competitor."[94]

Many associations hamper membership growth because they are operating with an antiquated membership model. Research shows that the majority of associations either have a single dues level that everyone pays, or very limited options (i.e., student membership or dues based on attributes like company size). It brings to mind Henry Ford's approach to standardizing his Model T for efficiency purposes by famously stating, "You can have any car color you want as long as it is black." The result was that Ford unwittingly provided an opportunity for General Motors to gain market share by offering customers a choice of car colors. Many associations find themselves in this same situation by essentially offering a "black Model T Ford" membership with no options on prices or the packages of benefits.

---

[93] Rossell, Wasserman, and Kerr, "The Membership Marketing Benchmarking Report, 12th Edition."
[94] "Product Line Extension - Oxford Reference."

> Launching new membership models has helped associations
> to respond to new market conditions, to offer members choices,
> and to allow for more competitively priced options.

As an alternative to those following a one-size-fits-all membership approach, associations that have updated their membership models by allowing prospects to select the option that best meets their needs and budgets have tapped into a significant growth opportunity. Launching new membership models has helped associations to respond to new market conditions, to offer members choices, and to allow for more competitively priced options. Benchmarking data supports the claim that adopting a new model gives a membership program a significant lift. Specifically, associations that have implemented a new model are 50 percent more likely to report an increase in the number of new members compared to those who have not. New membership models that have proven particularly effective include versions of either a combination membership or a tiered membership approach.

Combination Membership

Traditionally, associations operate either as an individual membership organization (IMO) or as a trade association with companies or organizations as their members. However, many IMOs are creating a hybrid model where they continue to make an individual membership available while also adding an institutional membership option. This hybrid model is called a combination membership. An association with a combination membership gives prospective members a choice to join as an individual (like a typical IMO) or to sign up their company or organization (like a typical trade association). It appears that the movement to embrace this model is growing. In the 2011 edition of the *Membership Marketing Benchmarking Report*, only 13 percent of respondents identified their association as having a combination structure. By 2020, 27 percent of respondents identified as a combination membership association. The combination structure also appears to be working. Combination membership associations have the highest median growth over the past five years.

One of the best examples of an association successfully moving to a combination membership model is the American Society of Association Executives (ASAE). For over 90 years, ASAE offered an individual membership. Over time, its membership grew to 23,000.

However, ASAE was only reaching a fraction of the staff employed in the association field. Working on the assumption that an association could improve its performance by giving its staff access to the knowledge and tools that ASAE provided, the association launched its combination model. While they continued to offer individual membership, ASAE provided the option of an organization membership that made services available to the entire staff of an association. They based dues levels on the number of full-time employees in the association. With this change, in just a few years, ASAE membership doubled, growing to 46,000 and providing the association with access to many more potential attendees and purchasers.

A scaled-down version of a combination membership is a departmental membership. With this model, instead of providing membership to all the staff in an organization, it serves a single department in an institution. The International Public Management Association for Human Resources (IPMA-HR) realized success by introducing this membership model. IPMA-HR serves government human resource agencies. Previously, prospects could choose between individual membership or group membership when joining IPMA-HR. The group membership was effectively a "bulk purchase" option offering a lower per-person cost for enrolling additional staff. However, IPMA-HR found that many times government entities were required to select the lowest dues option available. This restriction resulted in very large HR departments selecting the membership option to provide services to only two or three staff members.

Like ASAE, IPMA-HR understood this was leaving a vacuum in increasing the knowledge and skills development of HR agencies. In particular, the IPMA-HR board was concerned about succession planning in government agencies if future leadership did not receive adequate training and support. As a result, IPMA-HR replaced the group membership model with a combination membership that served the entire professional HR department within a government agency. Dues were based not on the number of staff the agency decided to enroll, but on the total number of HR professionals at the location. Under this model, all the professional HR staff were able to participate in the association as members. After adopting this new membership model, IPMA-HR witnessed a 25 percent growth in membership in the first year of its new departmental membership model.

Tiered Membership Models

The other successful membership model that associations have moved to is a tiered membership structure. This option has been the most popular, in the last five years, among those associations who have reported a change in their membership model. A tiered membership is not based on attributes of individuals or organizations; instead, it allows members to choose the option that best satisfies their needs and budget. One way to view a tiered membership model is to think of it as offering silver, gold, and platinum membership levels.

Associations offering a tiered membership structure maximize their revenue by allowing members to step into the level that they desire.

Tiered membership speaks to typical psychological buying patterns. Some people will always want the top of the line car, wine, or computer. At the same time, some consumers are budget conscious and will choose the least expensive or basic product or service. Associations offering a tiered membership structure maximize their revenue by allowing members to step into the level that they desire. Most associations have highly committed members who want access to almost everything an association produces. These are candidates for the top or premium membership level. There are others on a budget who want a no-frills option. The basic membership might be perfect for them and provide them with an attractive alternative to join or continue with the association.

For many associations, adopting a tiered structure does not require the development of entirely new products and services to be added for these new membership levels. Most associations who move to this model repackage the products that they already have available; however, instead of selling them independently, they incorporate them into the top membership levels. For example, an association might usually charge members for webinars, but be able to provide them at no additional cost to those at the premium level. Other organizations, as we will see, include a selection of the books they publish as part of a membership tier. They increase the press run to accommodate the premium members. And, by putting the books in the hands of these influential members, they find that they drive additional sales of the books to non-members. Interestingly, associations that have established a tiered structure find that members at the premium tier, in addition to the services included in the membership, are typically the top purchasers of other products. They also usually maintain the highest renewal rate.

Tiered membership, however, is not an "a la carte" membership. A totally customized benefits package is complicated to implement and would likely increase servicing costs. Instead, a tiered structure offers a series of defined membership packages from which a prospect can choose their preferred option.

Many organizations have implemented a tiered structure, from state-based associations like Colorado Veterinary Medical Association (CVMA) which offers Premium, Core, and Basic Membership to large national groups like the National Association for the Education of Young Children (NAEYC).

The NAEYC tiered membership structure includes three levels: Entry, Standard, and Premium membership.[95] For $30, Entry membership is digitally based. At this level, members can access the association publications and content online, and they can also participate in the private social network. At the Entry level, they also enjoy a 20 percent discount on NAEYC's online store.

The NAEYC Standard membership is where most of the members can be found. This level has a $69 dues rate and adds a print subscription to one of NAEYC's periodicals. Additionally, this membership level provides a complimentary NAEYC book selected by the association and complimentary registration for an online professional learning course.

NAEYC Premium members have a dues rate of $150 and receive all the benefits at the Entry and Standard levels plus:

- Print subscriptions to both of NAEYC's periodicals;
- Four complimentary books, as well as a coupon towards the purchase of a publication of their choice;
- Complimentary registration for two NAEYC online professional learning courses; and
- Access to VIP events, such as book signings and networking sessions, at NAEYC's Annual Conference.

A tiered structure can also be a practical membership growth innovation for trade associations. The National Business Aviation Association (NBAA) serves companies in the business aviation industry. They serve over 11,000 companies with their basic membership offer, with annual dues starting as low as $225. In addition to the basic membership, the association launched a new tier of membership that they called the NBAA Leadership Council. The Leadership Council offers several levels of participation, ranging from $10,000 to $50,000.

Members of the council receive recognition for their participation. They are acknowledged for their support at NBAA events and in listings

---

[95] "Member Benefits | NAEYC."

in NBAA's journal, on the website, and in the association's directory. They also receive additional registrations for meetings and invitations to receptions and political briefings on the state of the industry.

However, the core value of these members is that the revenue helps NBAA to advocate for business aviation. Dues help support the NBAA public awareness campaigns focused on changing perceptions about business aviation with policymakers and opinion leaders. The Leadership Council support also helps NBAA advocate against attempts to limit business aviation's access to airports and airspace.

Shortly after its launch, the Leadership Council reached 100 members and produced over $1 million in revenue for NBAA. And since the publications, website, and meetings where NBAA offers recognition to members was already in place, the additional cost to serve these members was limited. The dues revenue was able to flow directly into NBAA's advocacy efforts.

MANAGING CHANGE

A change like reaching out to a new market or launching a new membership model will meet with some challenges. Bringing in members from new markets can threaten the status quo and disrupt the "old boys' network." Volunteers may fight the revision of a pet program. IT staff may resist the work required to add new membership categories to the database and website.

However, there are some practices to make change easier. Perhaps the most important is to communicate and answer the most pressing question anyone confronted with change will ask: why? Any significant shift in our personal or professional life requires an adequate answer to why it is necessary. Before launching a change initiative, take the time to create a communications plan that speaks to all the constituencies that the change will impact. The message may vary depending on if you are talking to staff, to members, or the public, but it needs to present a clear vision of why the new direction is required and how things will be better because of the change.

Another method to build support for change is to identify champions and advocates willing to join you in innovating. Work with them to make sure each advocate understands and can present a unified change message. Together, your team can help build enthusiasm and excitement around a transition.

Finally, establish a schedule to implement the change with clear accountability outlined. No matter how well you communicate and have the support of your team, some people needed in the change process can require additional support or even become roadblocks and delay progress. With a step-by-step timetable in place, you can identify delays early on and provide the necessary guidance and resources to keep the process moving forward.

There is a reason that the term "innovate or die" is a constant theme in business literature. The markets that associations serve are changing, and associations need to innovate to continue to grow and thrive. Innovation has become a requirement and not an option. For associations, coupling innovation with a full-featured membership marketing program has proven to be an optimal combination for sustained growth.

CHAPTER TWELVE

WORDS OF WISDOM

There is an ancient proverb that says, "Without counsel plans fail, but with many advisers, they succeed."[96] I think this proverb effectively sums up my goal in writing this book. Chapter by chapter, I have shared what I have learned over the years in working with hundreds of membership professionals and many outstanding colleagues. Additionally, I have sought to draw on the insights from both contemporary membership experts and accomplished marketers from the past and present. And, finally, in this chapter, I want to highlight the words of wisdom that have been generously shared with me by association executives over the past several years through the membership marketing research we have conducted.

So here, organized by general topic area, is the advice and guidance from the hard-working association professionals who are daily engaged in growing their organizations' membership.

PLAN AND INVEST

A consistent theme from membership professionals is keeping the big picture in mind by establishing a plan and investing in recruitment. Membership professionals accomplished this goal by understanding the economics of membership that supports the program.

"You must have a multi-year strategic plan and actively pursue it." This plan includes "making the investment to market to your current and future members and measure results with the lifetime value of

---

96 Proverbs 15:22 ESV -The Holy Bible, English Standard Version. ESV® Text Edition: 2016. Copyright ©2001 by Crossway Bibles, a Publishing Ministry of Good News Publishers.

*the member." In short, "you have to invest resources in marketing
if you want a return of increased membership."*

*"You've got to spend money to recruit new members and retain
current members. You cannot expect to come out ahead the first or
second year. In fact, it may take two to three years or more before
you reap the benefits of your efforts."*

*"Membership is not a sprint. It's a long process that needs constant
attention."*

WORK AS A TEAM

The responsibility to grow membership does not fall on a single
individual. To succeed, the association's membership director needs
support and cooperation. An effective program requires the participation
of staff, volunteers, and dedicated members.

*"Membership marketing should be pervasive to the organization.
All staff and all volunteers are responsible for membership
marketing all year long and in every encounter with a member or
potential member." This involvement means that "we can no longer
have a 'build it and they will come' attitude about membership
recruitment."*

*"Every single employee must buy into a culture of sales. We all must
sell who we are and what we do."*

CAPITALIZE ON THE POWER OF INCENTIVES

As I have related earlier in this book, membership is a push product. It
is not a top-of-mind product that prospects seek out. It must be marketed
and offering an incentive to join is typically required to encourage
response.

*"Any kind of promotion or discount has moved those on the fence
to commit. Waive an enrollment fee, give a free gift with sign up, or
get in before the price goes up."*

Associations have tested many special offers to encourage prospects to join.

"We have tested a 15-months-for-the-price-of-12 against a straight $15 discount. Even though the former promotion is worth more to the member, the $15 off promo is much more successful. It appears to be the immediacy effect that makes this the offer to beat."

"One of the most successful new-member acquisitions is waiving the $65 initiation fee for the first year. That helps reduce some of the 'sticker shock' when a new member joins online and sees what the final cost of membership will be."

"We have had great success with Cyber Monday discounts on membership."

The consistent recommendation about using an incentive in recruitment is then to engage new members once they join.

"We discounted membership for the first year (try us out), but you have to be extremely careful that you are going to keep them engaged for that year with a robust welcome program, valuable benefits and services, and an emphasis on free things that they can get with their membership."

USE ALL OF THE TOOLS
AVAILABLE FOR RECRUITMENT

Perhaps the predominant theme shared in our research related to marketing channels is the need to learn what methods or combinations of methods work best in your marketplace. Over the last number of years, the possible ways to communicate with prospective members have widened. New technologies can be powerful tools, but so can the timeless methods of personal outreach.

"Multiple marketing channels are necessary because different people respond differently to each type of marketing channel. No one size fits all. Some people like phone calls, some emails, some prefer social media."

"Print mailers still grab attention. You need to diversify your marketing efforts to reach all audiences. Done right—direct mail for membership marketing is awesome."

"Telemarketing has significantly increased conversion rates. We have a ready database of potential members, available every month, and have refined and streamlined our contact with them. Conversion rates for telemarketing are around 15 percent."

"We increased Facebook and LinkedIn ads over the year as we were very successful in click-through rates and increasing membership."

"We send 3 direct mail pieces a year and have started to pair each campaign with Facebook ads targeting our internal segments. This has helped expand the reach of each campaign."

"Texting has been a recent boon for us. It's straightforward, to the point, and low cost."

"The more personal the outreach, the better. Handwritten note cards along with a gift or resource in the mail have worked very well for us."

"Person-to-person, peer-to-peer asking is still the most powerful. All the electronic methods reinforce these tactics, but rarely produce great results on their own."

"We are focused on training the chapter leaders who are recruiting the membership candidates through face-to-face contact."

ESTABLISH COMPELLING
RECRUITMENT COMMUNICATIONS

Association professionals have strong opinions on how to communicate with potential members. Maintaining consistency and frequency of communication is very important for recruiting members.

"People mostly do not join because no one has explained the benefits and asked them to join. If you never ask them to join, they won't join." So, *"you have to tell them your message multiple times*

before they start to get it. People are so distracted by the glut of information available and they don't have time to read it and process it all so you can't assume that they'll read your one communication."

"If you want to get their attention and get them to read your communications, you need to keep them short, succinct, and to the point."

"Stop listing off all of the specific programs that your organization does. Instead, focus on relaying how what we do will help them. They need to know that membership will help them in their careers."

Use *"testimonials from members to highlight why they choose to be a member."*

TEST AND TRACK EVERYTHING

Membership marketing professionals overwhelmingly underscore the importance of testing and tracking the results of their efforts, despite the challenges this may involve. By default, every marketing program will ultimately underperform unless mechanisms are in place to try new strategies and evaluate how well they work.

"You can't improve something if you don't measure it. Track everything. Statistics are our friends."

"The most important lesson we've learned in regard to membership marketing would be the importance of testing. You have to test everything, and you have to be able to consistently track responses to accurately determine if you're doing the right things to advance your membership marketing efforts."

"Relying on anecdotal data and ad hoc recruitment activities do not achieve membership growth."

"Don't keep doing the same things and expect different results. Take risks. Learn from mistakes and victories."

"What worked last year may not be the same thing that works this year. You always have to be looking for new ways to reach and engage members."

GOING FORWARD

Will membership associations thrive and remain relevant in the decades to come? Many would propose that the answer is "no." They see social divisions, technology, and economic restructuring as forces that will gradually cause the decline of this type of community. Indeed, these are challenges that associations will need to face and overcome. However, the very forces that threaten associations can also become the drivers for association success.

If people become disconnected from others, many of them will seek a community from an association where they can find like-minded individuals. As technology advances, associations can harness it for more effective marketing and member engagement. And as economic challenges present themselves, associations can provide the training to improve members' skills and provide efficient networks and meetings for businesses and customers.

In short, associations fulfill a crucial role in helping individuals and companies to connect, collaborate, and compete. And, understanding how to acquire members remains the core competency for achieving ongoing success.

ABOUT THE AUTHOR

Tony Rossell serves as the senior vice president of Marketing General Incorporated (MGI), a direct marketing agency in Alexandria, Virginia. For over three decades, he has consulted with hundreds of associations to help them achieve their membership growth goals and mission through better strategy, research, and marketing.

A frequent writer and speaker on marketing topics, Tony is a contributing author to two books, *Membership Marketing* (ASAE 2000) and *Membership Essentials* (Wiley 2016). He is a regular speaker at association conferences and has presented on membership marketing topics on four continents. He is the past chair of the ASAE Membership Professional Advisory Council. In his work at MGI, Tony launched the annual *Membership Marketing Benchmarking Report* and developed the membership framework he calls the "Membership Lifecycle."

In his free time, Tony loves spending time with his family, gardening, and hiking.

BIBLIOGRAPHY

The Ecommerce Expert. "22 Emotional Drivers That Influence Consumer Buying Behavior," August 25, 2009. https://www.theecommerceexpert.com/consumer-buying-emotional-drivers/.

Fortune. "Amazon Prime Has 100 Million U.S. Members." Accessed July 9, 2019. https://fortune.com/2019/01/17/amazon-prime-subscribers/.

"ASCD Annual Report." Annual Report, http://www.ascd.org/about-ascd/annual-report.aspx

Special Libraries Association. "Association Finances." Accessed October 25, 2019. https://www.sla.org/about-sla/association-finances/.

Associations Now. "Auto-Renewal and Monthly Payments: The Perfect Mix?," June 17, 2015. https://associationsnow.com/2015/06/auto-renewal-and-monthly-payments-the-perfect-mix/.

Baxter, Robbie Kellman. *The Forever Transaction.* New York: McGraw-Hill, 2020.

———. *The Membership Economy: Find Your Superusers, Master the Forever Transaction, and Build Recurring Revenue.* New York: McGraw-Hill Education, 2015.

Bly, Robert W. *The Direct Mail Revolution: How to Create Profitable Direct Mail Campaigns in a Digital World.* Irvine, California: Entrepreneur Press, 2019.

Carol Cohen, and Elisa Joseph. "Membership CPR: From Flagging to Thriving in Just 5 Years." Presented at the ASAE Annual Meeting, ASAE Annual Meeting Case Study Presentation August 11, 2019, n.d.

Federal Trade Commission. "Controlling the Assault of Non-Solicited Pornography and Marketing Act of 2003 (CAN-SPAM Act)," November 28, 2018. https://www.ftc.gov/enforcement/statutes/controlling-assault-non-solicited-pornography-marketing-act-2003-can-spam-act.

Statista. "Costco Membership Worldwide 2018." Accessed July 9, 2019. https://www.statista.com/statistics/718406/costco-membership/.

Dalton, James G, Monica Dignam, American Society of Association Executives, and Center for Association Leadership. *The Decision to Join: How Individuals Determine Value and Why They Choose to Belong.* Washington, D.C.: ASAE & the Center for Association Leadership, 2007.

thedma.org. "DMAChoice - Do Not Mail List - Direct Mail Preference Service." Accessed August 16, 2019. https://thedma.org/accountability/dma-choice/.

Editors, History com. "Alexis de Tocqueville." HISTORY. Accessed July 9, 2019. https://www.history.com/topics/france/alexis-de-tocqueville.

"EUGDPR – Information Portal." Accessed August 16, 2019. https://eugdpr.org/.

"Five Reasons Why Membership Is Killing Association Business Models by Jeff De Cagna FRSA FASAE." Accessed July 9, 2019. http://www.csae.com/Portals/0/Events/Handouts/Jeff%20De%20Cagna%20-%205%20%20Reasons%20Why%20M'ship%20is%20Killing%20Association%20Business%20Models.pdf.

Galvin, John. "Harley Owners Group 30th Anniversary Celebration: Riding with a Passion," November 27, 2013. https://thunderpress.net/top-stories/harley-owners-group-30th-anniversary-celebration/2013/11/27.htm.

Geller, Lois K. *Response: The Complete Guide to Profitable Direct Marketing.* Rev. and Expanded ed. Oxford; New York: Oxford University Press, 2002.

Godin, Seth. *This Is Marketing: You Can't Be Seen until You Learn to See.* London: Portfolio Penguin, 2018.

Government of Canada, Canadian Radio-television and Telecommunications Commission (CRTC). "Canada's Anti-Spam Legislation." Consumer information, October 24, 2013. https://crtc.gc.ca/eng/internet/anti.htm.

Public Relations Society of America. "Group Membership." Accessed August 10, 2019. https://www.prsa.org/membership/group-membership/.

"HigherLogic_Report_Association Email Marketing Benchmark Report 2017.Pdf." Accessed August 16, 2019. https://resources.higherlogic.com/hubfs/Marketing%20Automation/MA_Resources/HigherLogic_Report_Association%20Email%20Marketing%20Benchmark%20Report%202017.pdf.

"History." Accessed November 29, 2019.
https://www.aaae.org/aaae/AAAEMBR/About/History/AAAE
MemberResponsive/About_AAAE/History.aspx?hkey=9d0f3525-
8a20-417e-b0be-66c7f68a5fab.

"H.O.G. Member Benefits | Harley-Davidson USA." Accessed July 9,
2019. https://www.harley-davidson.com#.

Hopkins, Claude C. *My Life in Advertising and Scientific Advertising*
(Advertising Age Classics Library): Claude C. Hopkins:
9780844231013: Amazon.Com: Gateway. Accessed June 23, 2019.
https://www.amazon.com/Life-Advertising-Scientific-Classics-
Library/dp/0844231010/ref=sr_1_3?crid=2XKCKCOXC5PVJ&key
words=scientific+advertising+by+claude+hopkins&qid=1561314109
&s=gateway&sprefix=Hopkins+scien%2Caps%2C144&sr=8-3.

"IEEE Member Referral Form | IEEE Forms." Accessed August 19,
2019. https://forms.vtools.ieee.org/ieee-member-referral-form/.

"Industries & Media Kits | SmartBrief." Accessed August 2, 2019.
https://www.smartbrief.com/about/advertising/industries#Education.

Associations Now. "Is Career Stage the Key to Member Acquisition?,"
July 31, 2018. https://associationsnow.com/2018/07/career-stage-key-
member-acquisition/.

Jacobs, Sheri, ed. *Membership Essentials: Recruitment, Retention, Roles,
Responsibilities, and Resources*. Second edition. Hoboken, New
Jersey: ASAE / Wiley, 2016.

Kahan, Seth. "6 Key Issues Facing Association Leaders." Fast Company,
April 12, 2013. https://www.fastcompany.com/3008159/6-key-issues-
facing-association-leaders.

Keller, Gary, and Jay Papasan. *The One Thing: The Surprisingly Simple
Truth behind Extraordinary Results*. Austin, Texas: Bard Press, 2013.

Kim, W. Chan, and Renée Mauborgne. *Blue Ocean Strategy: How to
Create Uncontested Market Space and Make the Competition
Irrelevant*. Expanded edition. Boston, Massachusetts: Harvard
Business Review Press, 2015.

Kotler, Philip. *Kotler on Marketing: How to Create, Win, and Dominate
Markets*. New York: Free Press, 1999.

Kotler, Philip, Hermawan Kartajaya, and Iwan Setiawan. *Marketing 4.0:
Moving from Traditional to Digital*. Hoboken, New Jersey: Wiley,
2017.

Leaning, Brittany. "31 Call-to-Action Examples You Can't Help But
Click." Accessed August 22, 2019.
https://blog.hubspot.com/marketing/call-to-action-examples.

Lisa Boylan. "Membership Success Stories Amid Covid-19."
Https://associationsnow.com/2020/06/membership-success-stories-

amid-covid-19/?utm_medium=email&utm_source=rasa_io. *Associatoions Now* (blog), n.d.

Associations Now. "Member Acquisition: Follow the ROI," October 11, 2017. https://associationsnow.com/2017/10/member-acquisition-follow-roi/.

"Member Benefits | NAEYC." Accessed January 17, 2020. https://www.naeyc.org/get-involved/membership/benefits.

Associations Now. "Membership Memo: The Hybrid Model," October 1, 2015. https://associationsnow.com/2015/10/membership-memo-hybrid-model/.

Memberships | Nintendo Switch Online | Nintendo. "Memberships | Nintendo Switch Online | Nintendo." Accessed July 9, 2019. https://ec.nintendo.com/US/en/membership.

NBAA - National Business Aviation Association. "NBAA Reaches 11,000-Member Mark," July 28, 2016. https://nbaa.org/press-releases/nbaa-reaches-11000-member-mark/.

The Hollywood Reporter. "Netflix Grows Subscriber Base to 139 Million Worldwide." Accessed July 9, 2019. https://www.hollywoodreporter.com/news/netflix-grows-subscriber-base-139-million-worldwide-1176934.

"Product Line Extension - Oxford Reference." Accessed December 31, 2019. https://www.oxfordreference.com/view/10.1093/oi/authority.2011080 3100348150.

Proverbs 15:22 ESV -The Holy Bible, English Standard Version. ESV® Text Edition: 2016. Copyright © 2001 by Crossway Bibles, a Publishing Ministry of Good News Publishers., n.d. Accessed September 27, 2019.

"Putnam, R. D. (1995). Bowling Alone: America's Declining Social Capital. Journal of Democracy 6 (1), 65-78. | Socialcapitalgateway.Org," June 26, 2011. http://www.socialcapitalgateway.org/content/paper/putnam-r-d-1995-bowling-alone-americas-declining-social-capital-journal-democracy-6-1-.

Randall, Chris, Alan Lewis, and Amanda Davis. "How Subscriptions Are Creating Winners and Losers in Retail." *Harvard Business Review*, January 8, 2016. https://hbr.org/2016/01/how-subscriptions-are-creating-winners-and-losers-in-retail.

Default. "Report of the Economic Survey." Accessed August 13, 2019. https://www.aipla.org/home/news-publications/economic-survey.

Ridley, Matt. *How Innovation Works: Serendipity, Energy and the Saving of Time.* S.l.: HarperCollins, 2020.

"Robert Putnam - Bowling Alone - Journal of Democracy 6:1." Accessed July 9, 2019. http://xroads.virginia.edu/~HYPER/DETOC/assoc/bowling.html.

Rossell, Tony, Adina Wasserman, and Matt Kerr. "The Membership Marketing Benchmarking Report, 12th Edition." Marketing General Knowledge Bank, April 20, 2020. https://www.marketinggeneral.com/knowledge-bank/.

Sheri Jacobs. *The Art of Membership: How to Attract, Retain and Cement Member Loyalty*. First edition. San Francisco, California: Jossey-Bass, 2014.

Sinek, Simon. *Start with Why: How Great Leaders Inspire Everyone to Take Action*. New York: Portfolio, 2009.

Sladek, Sarah L. *End of Membership as We Know It - Building the Fortune-Flipping, Must-Have.*, 2011.

"Society for Human Resource Management." In *Wikipedia*, July 1, 2019. https://en.wikipedia.org/w/index.php?title=Society_for_Human_Resource_Management&oldid=904391848.

Stone, Bob. *Successful Direct Marketing Methods*. 6th ed. Lincolnwood, Ill: NTC Business Books, 1997.

"The AOPA Sweepstakes." Text, March 7, 2019. https://www.aopa.org/membership/sweeps.

"The Empire Called AARP Under Its Nonprofit Halo, the American Association of Retired Persons Is a Feared Lobbyist and an Even More Awesome Marketer. - October 1, 1988." Accessed December 6, 2019. https://money.cnn.com/magazines/moneymag/moneymag_archive/1988/10/01/84702/index.htm.

"The History of Communication Technology." Accessed August 14, 2019. https://www.conferencecallsunlimited.com/history-of-communication-technology/.

"The Minty Fresh Psychology Behind America's Toothpaste Obsession." Accessed September 13, 2019. https://heleo.com/charles-duhigg-the-minty-fresh-psychology-behind-americas-toothpaste-obsession/1196/.

Small Business. "The One Letter That Generated $1.5 Billion in Revenues." Accessed November 15, 2019. https://smallbusiness.yahoo.com/advisor/one-letter-generated-1-5-billion-revenues-013020140.html.

"The Quest for Resilience." Accessed October 11, 2019. https://hbr.org/2003/09/the-quest-for-resilience.

Consumer Information. "The Telemarketing Sales Rule," August 5, 2016. https://www.consumer.ftc.gov/articles/0198-telemarketing-sales-rule.

Tocqueville, Alexis de, and Henry Reeve. *Democracy in America*. A Bantam Classic. New York: Bantam Books, 2000.

BrainyQuote. "Tom Peters Quotes." Accessed August 1, 2019. https://www.brainyquote.com/authors/tom-peters-quotes.

"W. Edwards Deming." In *Wikipedia*, August 15, 2019. https://en.wikipedia.org/w/index.php?title=W._Edwards_Deming&oldid=911001709.

BusinessDictionary.com. "What Is 40 40 20 Rule? Definition and Meaning." Accessed August 2, 2019. http://www.businessdictionary.com/definition/40-40-20-rule.html.

"Whiteford Taylor Preston, LLP | Automatic Renewal of Membership Dues and Recurring Credit Card Payment Laws." Accessed August 13, 2019. https://www.wtplaw.com/news-events/automatic-renewal-of-membership-dues-and-recurring-credit-card-payment-laws.

"Why ASQ? | ASQ." Accessed August 21, 2019. https://asq.org/why-asq.

"Winning Back Lost Customers." *Harvard Business Review*, March 1, 2016. https://hbr.org/2016/03/winning-back-lost-customers.

SHRM. "World's Largest HR Association Reaches Quarter Million Members," November 6, 2008. https://www.shrm.org/about-shrm/press-room/press-releases/pages/worldslargesthrassociation reachesquartermillionmembers.aspx.

Personify Corp. "Young Members 2.0." Accessed August 22, 2019. https://personifycorp.com/resources/gated/download-young-members.

Made in the USA
Monee, IL
26 April 2021